HEAR G

HEAR GOD'S VOICE

DEREK PRINCE

© 2020 by Derek Prince Ministries–International
This edition DPM-UK 2021

ISBN 978-1-78263-738-7
ePub 978-1-78263-739-4
Kindle 978-1-78263-740-0

Book code B136

Publisher's note: This book was compiled from the extensive archive of Derek
Prince's unpublished materials and approved by the Derek Prince Ministries
editorial team.

Derek Prince Ministries · www.derekprince.com

Set in Arno Pro by Raphael Freeman MISTD, Renana Typesetting

Contents

FOREWORD

The Wonder of Hearing God's Voice

How important is it to hear God's voice – beyond what we read in the Bible? Would you say that you are able to hear God speak to you? What price would you be willing to pay to clearly hear His voice?

Many biblical themes can be taught in a straight-forward manner, but the matter of hearing God's voice is necessarily subjective. This is not to say the Bible doesn't guide us in knowing God's will and learning to discern His voice. But specific answers to many of our questions in life are not always directly available in the Scriptures. For those questions, we need to receive personal guidance from the Lord. One principle is clear: we must take responsibility for making time not only to listen to, but also to test, what we hear spiritually. No one else can do this for us.

Nothing is more important to our spiritual life than learning to hear God's voice. Derek Prince learned much about this ability through his study of the Scriptures and through his own experiences. As he did with many other biblical subjects, early in his ministry, Derek taught extensively and effectively on this topic. Then, in his later years, he gained additional wisdom and personal experience – sometimes through the tests and trials he describes in this book. Consequently, the Lord refined and deepened his understanding of this message.

As you read the teachings Derek shares in *Hear God's Voice*, we hope the importance of hearing the Lord's voice for yourself will become clear and that experiencing this wonder will become more accessible to you. As you put these principles and skills into practice in your daily walk of faith, we pray that your life will be transformed and your fellowship with Jesus Christ will be revitalized.

– THE INTERNATIONAL PUBLISHING TEAM
OF DEREK PRINCE MINISTRIES

PART I
Our Sovereign God

ONE

Taking Time to Hear

I want to begin *Hear God's Voice* by sharing an experience my wife Ruth and I had some years ago. We took a "sabbatical" of six months that turned out to be one of the most intense and challenging times of our lives. Although the experience was very difficult, it ended up being the means by which we eventually heard God's voice and discovered His life-changing direction for us.

TRIALS AND TESTING

Ruth and I had both felt the Lord was leading us to take an extended rest from our ministry work. We planned a sabbatical in Hawaii because we wanted to hear from God and learn what He was asking us to do next. We felt we had come to the end of the current phase of our ministry, and, naturally, we wanted to know God's purposes for us.

When we arrived in Hawaii, we had great expectations of having a wonderful respite in a warm climate surrounded by the Pacific Ocean. We thought this six-month break would be relaxing and restful, with plenty of time to read the Bible, pray, and walk by the ocean and on the beautiful hills. But it didn't turn out like that at all!

I started to feel unwell, and I became increasingly sick. At first, the doctors couldn't determine what was wrong with me. Eventually, I was diagnosed with what is called subacute bacterial endocarditis, which is a progressive infection of the lining of the heart. I ended up spending seventeen days in the hospital and six weeks on intravenous antibiotics.

In addition to this situation, a few months earlier, Ruth had faced a life-threatening illness. It had started when she and I were in New Zealand for meetings with our international directors. Ruth began having intense abdominal pain, and I didn't know what to do. But when she began praying, "Lord, I commit the family to you," and then, "Lord, I commit the ministry to you," and then, "Lord, I commit Derek to you," it got my attention. I thought to myself, "I had better do something quickly!"

I phoned the Derek Prince Ministries directors who were staying at the same meeting place in New Zealand, and they immediately came and prayed. Thankfully,

Ruth was raised up. But I felt she really had been at death's door.

A NEW SEASON

In preparation for our time away in Hawaii, I had handed over the administration of the ministry to my son-in-law. Taking six months away from the ministry seemed like a very long time to us. Yet, we believed that by consecrating this period to the Lord, we would receive new direction. Our thought was, "If we give Him six months, that will be wonderful."

Rather ironically, we heard nothing from God about our future until almost the end of those six months. The Lord spent all that time dealing with problems in us that were preventing us from being ready to hear and respond to what He had to say.

Usually, if a preacher speaks about personal problems, most people tend to conclude the issue is one of the following: immorality, alcohol abuse, or misappropriation of funds. In our case, it was none of these! As you might guess, there are plenty of other ways Christians can block God's purpose for their lives. God dealt with some of those issues during our sabbatical – clearing them away so we could more clearly hear from Him. He used our trials to chasten and refine us for His service.

GOD'S CHASTENING

As you may be aware, just before I start teaching in front of a congregation or audience, Ruth and I usually make a confession or proclamation from Scripture out loud. Speaking God's Word has a very powerful effect on the spiritual atmosphere; it sets the scene for the Lord to work through the message that is given.

One of the passages I have learned by heart for this purpose is Psalm 118:13–18. God has used these verses to accelerate my thinking and experience in regard to the way He works to purify us.

> *You [the psalmist's enemy] pushed me violently, that I might fall, but the Lord helped me. The Lord is my strength and song, and He has become my salvation. The voice of rejoicing and salvation is in the tents of the righteous; the right hand of the Lord does valiantly. The right hand of the Lord is exalted; the right hand of the Lord does valiantly. I shall not die, but live, and declare the works of the Lord. The Lord has chastened me severely, but He has not given me over to death.*
>
> (Psalm 118:13–18)

The Bible tells us, "For whom the Lord loves He chastens" (Hebrews 12:6). How do you regard the Lord's chastening? By biblical standards, if I am a person without chastening, I am not a true child of God. Rather, I am someone who is referred to as "illegitimate."

I have a deep concern for the vast majority of Christians because they do not make any place for God's chastening. Some actually resist His correction and redirection in their lives. Consequently, they may not be where they ought to be in their relationship with the Lord. They may not be hearing His voice.

What about you? Do you need help to get onto the right path with the Lord? I can assure you that my desire in writing this book is not to accuse or condemn you but to help you.

A LIFESAVING TRIAL

After Ruth and I had come through this period of testing and struggle, a dear brother in the Lord said to me, "Your decision to take a sabbatical saved your life. If you had continued traveling and ministering, you probably would not have had the opportunity to have the close medical supervision that eventually uncovered your problem. You might have died."

So, I want to express that if you go on being as busy as you are, with as little time for waiting on God as you have allowed, you might jeopardize your future. The gospel is a serious message. It is a message of life and death – and we have to be just as serious in our response to it. We need to take time to hear God's voice.

TWO

Are You Prepared to Wait?

As difficult as that long sabbatical was for Ruth and me, the direction we received after waiting to hear from the Lord was very simple and practical. God showed us that, from then on, our ministry was to focus on intercession, prayer, worship, and waiting upon Him. He also revealed the place that was to be our base for this ministry: our home in Jerusalem.

If we had allotted the Lord only five months to hear from Him, we might not have received the answer to our questions. As I previously explained, for five and a half months, God didn't tell us anything specific about what we should do next. He spoke to us about other matters, but not what He wanted us to do for Him in the future.

It was only in the last two weeks that God gave us His answers to our question, "What do You want us to do, Lord?" We learned many lessons during this period of waiting, but the first lesson was this: God wants our time. If we are not prepared to give Him our time, I don't think we can expect to hear from Him.

I have learned by experience – and the Lord has confirmed this truth in many ways – that He wants open-ended time with us. He doesn't want us to say, "Lord, I'll give You the next half hour" – or even an hour or even half a day. Instead, He is seeking this affirmation from us: "Lord, I'll give You all the time it takes until I hear from You, no matter how long." It is tremendously important that we open up our time to the Lord in this way. I recognize that most people couldn't take six months off from their job or other responsibilities; but we can make other time available to seek God's voice and receive His direction. For example, we might set aside a portion of time each day to worship Him and pray for His guidance. Or, we might devote a certain amount of time on the weekend for this purpose.

MEETING GOD'S CONDITIONS

Would you love to hear from God? Perhaps you have been asking the Lord to speak to you, but you haven't heard anything from Him. The reason may be that you are not meeting His conditions. God has wonderful plans for you and me. His plans may be totally different from what we anticipate. But we will never discover them unless we hear from Him. So, actively listening for and hearing God's voice are absolute priorities for us.

WHY THE NEED TO WAIT?

You might ask, "Why did you and Ruth have to wait five and a half months to hear from God?" I will provide two answers to that question.

First of all, God is sovereign. This truth is hardly ever mentioned in the church today. Here is my definition of God's sovereignty: God does what He wants to, when He wants to, the way He wants to, and He asks no one's permission. If we haven't yet learned this truth, then we have a very important lesson to learn. We cannot dictate a time frame to God. He alone decides when we will hear from Him.

The second reason why we had to wait was practical; as I explained, we needed to remove the barriers in our lives. As God revealed these barriers to us, we discovered there were many obstacles within us that were blocking the way. These hindrances had to be removed before the Lord could have His way in our lives and we could hear His instruction. It took those five and a half months for us to deal with what He had shown us.

Once more, so that you don't get the wrong impression, please understand I'm not talking about sins such as sexual immorality or drunkenness. Those were not the types of sins God dealt with in Ruth and me. In a sense, it really doesn't matter which sin we are contending with. Any sin can hinder us from hearing from the Lord.

SELF-HUMBLING

The way God required us to remove the barriers was by confession of the sins He had showed us, repentance, and self-humbling. In many ways, I really believe the key is self-humbling.

Somebody once said, "Humility is not something you are; humility is something you do." If you simply "try" to feel humble, you will never achieve humility. Do what humility dictates, and the results will follow.

Waiting on the Lord and humility are two of the requirements for hearing from God that we will explore later in this book. But, first, we must understand the importance of our relationship to the Head in the body of Christ to be in a proper position to hear God's voice.

THREE

The Importance of Christ as Our Head

As we begin to look at what the Scriptures say concerning hearing God's voice, I want to focus on a foundational principle I believe has been radically displaced in the church. I am not saying it has been neglected among every group of Christians, but it has in most groups. I am referring to the need for a clear understanding of – and reverence toward – an indispensable part of the body of Christ – the Head.

A MOST WONDERFUL GIFT

[God] put all things under [Jesus's] feet, and gave Him to be head over all things to the church, which is His body. (Ephesians 1:22–23)

In this verse, there is an interesting contrast in language. On the one hand, "[God] put all things under

[Jesus's] feet" – everything was subjected to Christ. On the other hand, God positioned Jesus as "head" of the church – the most wonderful gift He could ever give us.

This gift of Jesus's headship was not for our sub-jection. It was not for our domination. Rather, it was a precious blessing from God for His people. And He made Jesus Head over all things. Not over a few things, and not even over most things – over all things.

If I were to ask if Jesus's headship is a reality in your life, could you honestly say it is so? Could you truly say in the presence of God that Jesus is Head over every-thing in your life? That there is nothing outside of His control and determined will for you?

DEPENDENCE UPON THE HEAD

In Ephesians 4:15–16, Paul writes more about the impor-tance of the Head to the body:

> But [we], speaking the truth in love [or being honest in love], may grow up in all things into Him who is the Head – Christ – from whom the whole body, joined and knit together by what every joint supplies, according to the effective working by which every part does its share, causes growth of the body for the edifying of itself in love.

Please notice the underlying truth of this passage: the whole body depends on the Head. It is only through its relationship to the Head that the body derives nourishment. It is only because of the Head that the body is able to grow and function effectively. If the connection to the Head is impaired, the entire life of the body is automatically impaired as well.

A LOST CONNECTION

Paul provides further instruction about the Head in Colossians 2. Let us begin by looking at verse 18:

Let no one cheat you of your reward....

Actually, this verse would be better translated as, "Let no one disqualify you from your reward." In other words, don't let anything or anyone cause you to lose what God intends you to have. To help us know what to watch out for, Paul goes on to describe the actions of the person who might try to defraud us:

Taking delight in false humility and worship of angels, intruding into those things which he has not seen, vainly puffed up by his fleshly mind....
(Colossians 2:18)

Paul describes a person who claims to be superspiritual but is actually very carnal. He warns that we should not let such a person deceive us and cheat us out of our rightful inheritance. Still speaking about this type of person, Paul says,

And not holding fast to the Head, from whom all the body, nourished and knit together by joints and ligaments, grows with the increase that is from God.
(Colossians 2:19)

In the New International Version, this verse begins, "They have lost connection with the head...." As soon as we lose connection with the Head, we make ourselves susceptible to error, deception, and all kinds of false teachings that are out of line with God's truth. We start listening to the wrong voices.

BEING RIGHTLY RELATED TO THE HEAD

The only position of safety for the body collectively – and for each believer individually – is to be rightly related to the Head. Every true believer has a direct, divinely prepared connection with Jesus Christ. Never let anyone interfere with your personal connection with the Head.

In the church, pastors are sometimes referred to as the head of the congregation. Pastors are wonderful people, but they cannot take the place of Jesus. The function of a pastor is not to be your head. His role is to help you cultivate your relationship with the One who is your Head. Your pastor's obligation is not to tell you the answers to all your problems, but rather to show you how to find the answers for yourself from Jesus.

Some people tend to be lazy, wanting another

human being to solve all their problems for them. Life is not designed to work that way. God wants us to be rightly connected to the Head, Jesus Christ, as our ultimate Source of everything we need.

Some leaders are despotic; they want to control other people. I have had personal experience with such situations. I thank God that I was able to remove myself from these circumstances. Believe me, I have no desire to be in that type of situation ever again.

We have been designed and created to have our own personal relationships with Jesus. Yet, in order to have an effective connection with Him, we have to be able to hear Him speak. We have to learn to be directed by Him. We must have the ability to discern when He is pleased and when He is displeased with us or something in our life. For this to happen, we continually need to be sensitive to the Head – Jesus Christ.

FOUR

Four Functions of the Head

As we continue to consider the importance of being aligned with the Lord Jesus Christ, let's look at four specific functions of a head. This is not a lesson in physiology. Instead, I want to present some simple, practical perspectives to help us relate properly to our spiritual Head. In my way of thinking, a head, or the Head, has four main functions:

1. To receive input. Every part of the body has a right to communicate with the head. The head receives all such communication.
2. To make decisions. The head decides what the body is to do.
3. To initiate actions. The head takes the initiative.
4. To coordinate the activity of the body. Having taken the initiative, the head organizes the members of the body that will accomplish the plan it has made.

THE ROLE OF THE HOLY SPIRIT

In the body of Christ, Jesus's headship is effective only through the Holy Spirit. The Spirit is the sole means by which Jesus can communicate with, direct, control, and preserve the body. Although our primary relationship is with Jesus, a relationship with the Holy Spirit, whom Jesus promised to be our Guide and Counselor, is an essential part of that connection.

Let me give you just one of many Scripture passages that confirm the vital role of the Holy Spirit in our lives. In John 16:12–13, Jesus said to His disciples:

> *I still have many things to say to you, but you cannot bear them now. However, when He, the Spirit of truth, has come, He will guide you into all truth.*

Jesus was saying, in effect, "I cannot tell you now everything you need to know. You are not in a condition to receive any more. In fact, you are already overwhelmed by what I have told you so far. But that does not matter because the Spirit of Truth – the Holy Spirit – is coming. He will guide you. He will take over for Me in directing you."

SOMEONE TO HELP US

It is interesting that the above translation of John 16:13 says, "When He, the Spirit of truth, has come...." The original text of this verse is in Greek, and in that language, there are three genders: masculine, feminine, and neuter (he, she, and it). Interestingly, the word pneuma, translated "Spirit," is neuter. So, the normal pronoun would be it. The rules of grammar are broken here by the use of the pronoun He. Why? To emphasize that the Holy Spirit is a Person. He is not just something; He is Someone. You can't rightly relate to the Holy Spirit if you merely regard Him as an it. He is a Person.

God the Father is a Person. Jesus Christ the Son is a Person. The Holy Spirit is a Person. In John 16:12–15, Jesus was indicating, "From this time forward, My relationship with you will be effected through the Holy Spirit – a Person."

SUPERNATURAL DIRECTION

Jesus continued His discourse to His disciples by saying,

For He [the Holy Spirit] will not speak on His own authority, but whatever He hears He will speak; and He will tell you things to come. (John 16:13)

The church needs supernatural direction concerning the future. How will it come to us? Through the Holy Spirit. He will not provide information regarding everything in our future, but He will tell us the things we need to know. My personal view of the world situation is that if the church goes into the future without the Holy Spirit's wisdom and knowledge to guide us, we are headed for disaster.

I believe that, up to this point, most of us have only

glimpsed the troubles and pressures that are coming upon the whole world. We will need the Holy Spirit to warn us of events that are going to happen so we can avoid being in the wrong place at the wrong time. One of the prayers that Ruth and I pray regularly is that we will always be in the right place at the right time. Only the Holy Spirit can make that possible.

GLORIFYING JESUS

In John 16:14, Jesus added this principle to His teaching on the Holy Spirit:

He [the Holy Spirit] will glorify Me....

Please note this primary, distinctive mark of the Holy Spirit: He glorifies Jesus. A number of activities and expressions in Christianity are said to be the work of the Holy Spirit. However, many of these activities and expressions lack the mark spoken of in this verse. They do not glorify Jesus.

Any activity or practice that exalts a human personality is not from the Holy Spirit. It may be spiritual, but it is not from the Holy Spirit. Please bear that in mind. Whatever the Holy Spirit does, His ultimate aim is always to glorify the Son. If Jesus is not at center stage, the scenario is not from the Holy Spirit.

So far in this book, we have seen our need to take time to wait on the Lord. We have also noted the importance of being in the right position in the body of Christ, with Jesus as our Head – the One who communicates, directs, controls, and preserves the church through the Holy Spirit. Our next step is to recognize that hearing from God is His invariable requirement for His people – one that has remained constant throughout the ages.

PART II
Ears to Hear

FIVE

God's Unvarying Requirement

The Bible reveals that, throughout human history, there have been periods when God has dealt with the human race in different ways. In some respects, He has changed His manner of interacting with humanity in succeeding eras. Dispensations is the theological word to describe this variety of authority – God's different dealings from one period to another.

In this chapter, I will point out certain facts about these dispensations – some of the ways in which they differ, along with one important way in which they are alike.

THREE DISPENSATIONS

The Bible depicts three main dispensations. The first is the dispensation of the Patriarchs. This term refers to the "fathers" of families – people like Abraham, Isaac, and Jacob. Even before these fathers, there were patriarchs like Enoch and Noah. In the period – or dispensation – of the fathers, God dealt primarily with individuals and with their families as they related directly to Him.

After the Patriarchs came the dispensation that is often called the Law. During this period, God began to deal specifically with Israel as a collective nation of people. He placed the Israelites under a special law that did not entirely apply to other nations. During most of the time of this dispensation, Israel had a temple and a priesthood. So, the outstanding features of this particular dispensation were the Law, the temple, and the priesthood.

The third dispensation is often called the Gospel. This period involves a proclamation to the whole of humanity, irrespective of race or nationality. It is the proclamation of the gospel of Jesus Christ, and it requires an individual response from each person.

To recap what we have just covered, throughout the Bible, we can discern three major dispensations: the Patriarchs (involving individuals and their families), the Law (focusing on Israel as a collective nation), and the Gospel (concerning the proclamation of the good news of Jesus Christ to the whole of humanity). We are still living in the third dispensation today.

As I expressed earlier, what God required of people within the various dispensations was somewhat different. However, in the midst of all the differences, there remained one unvarying requirement – one response that God has always mandated.

Can you guess the answer I have in mind? Do you know what the one requirement is? I believe it is vital for us not only to know what this unvarying requirement is, but also to see how it has never changed from dispensation to dispensation. What is the requirement? To hear God's voice.

Undoubtedly, hearing God's voice is what has always distinguished those who belong to the Lord. It is the quality that has made them different from all other people.

THE IMPORTANCE OF HEARING GOD'S VOICE

Let's now look at some examples from the Pentateuch, the first five books of the Bible, demonstrating the singular importance of hearing God's voice:

"IF YOU WILL DILIGENTLY HEED"

The first example is from Exodus 15. After being freed from slavery in Egypt, the Israelites had come to a point in their journey through the wilderness where they were very thirsty. In that condition, they came upon a pool of water. However, the people could not drink from that pool because it was bitter, so they called it Marah, or "Bitter."

Faced with this situation, Moses prayed to the Lord, who showed him a certain tree and revealed what action to take with it. When Moses cast the tree into the pool, its waters were made sweet, and the people could drink from it. In the context of this miraculous event, the Lord said to the Israelites,

> *If you diligently heed the voice of the Lord your God and do what is right in His sight, give ear to His commandments and keep all His statutes, I will put none of the diseases on you which I have brought on the Egyptians. For I am the Lord who heals you.*
> (Exodus 15:26)

What was the primary requirement? "If you diligently heed the voice of the Lord your God." In the Hebrew language, the phrase translated "If you diligently heed" means "If you will listen, listening." I interpret that to mean that we have to listen to God's voice with both of our ears – the right and the left. God says to the Israelites, "If you will listen in this way, you will never be sick. I will keep you healthy. I will be your doctor. I will accept responsibility for your physical well-being."

Early in my life, there was a time when I was sick in the hospital and the doctors could not heal me. So, I had to seek God regarding how I could receive healing from Him. As I studied the Scriptures in this context, I discovered that in almost every place where God speaks about our being healed, the emphasis is on what we listen to. We find the same emphasis in this passage: "If you diligently heed the voice of the Lord your God…, I will put none of [these] diseases on you."

I believe this promise is still true today. Those who learn to listen to God with both ears – hearing His voice and obeying Him – can lead a life that is free from sickness and many other plagues and problems. And, as I described earlier, when we do experience sickness and trials as we seek to hear His voice, it causes us to press in to Him even more to discover His will and plans for us.

"IF YOU WILL INDEED OBEY"

Another example that shows us the importance of hearing God's voice is in Exodus 19. In this incident, the Israelites came to the foot of Mount Sinai, and Moses went up the mountain to have an encounter with the Lord. During that meeting, God spoke to Moses and gave him this message for the children of Israel:

> *Thus you shall say to the house of Jacob, and tell the children of Israel: "You have seen what I did to the Egyptians, and how I bore you on eagles' wings and brought you to Myself. Now therefore, if you*

will indeed obey My voice and keep My covenant,
then you shall be a special treasure to Me above all
people; for all the earth is Mine. And you shall be to
Me a kingdom of priests and a holy nation." These
are the words which you shall speak to the children
of Israel. (Exodus 19:3–6)

Again, please notice what the first condition is: "If
you will obey My voice, then My will shall be worked
out for you. You will be a unique people, different from
all others. You will be able to live on a higher level, experiencing a measure of provision and blessing unknown
to other people." But here is the primary requirement:
"If you will indeed obey My voice."

I would like to point out four phases of God's dealings with Israel as revealed in the passage from Exodus
19:

First, the Lord says He brought Israel to Himself.
That is always the primary purpose of redemption – for
us to come to God personally.

Second, He says, "I want you to obey My voice."
Our acts of obedience are what lead us into God's provision.

Third, the Lord says, "If you will keep My covenant."
The way God settles and finalizes His relationship with
His people is by way of His covenant with them, which
we must recognize and honor.

Fourth, He says, "You will be a kingdom of priests

and a holy nation." God's intention for us is to be a unique people, blessed above all other peoples, distinct from all other peoples.

Thus, here is the order in which we are to respond to God: come to Him, obey His voice, keep His covenant, and, thereby, become a kingdom of priests and a holy nation.

"IF YOU WILL DILIGENTLY OBEY"

Let us move on to the fifth book of the Pentateuch to see a different context for the same requirement of hearing God's voice. Deuteronomy 28 records Moses's instructions to the Israelites just before they entered their inheritance in the land of Canaan, the promised land. These instructions were a recapitulation of God's commands for the nation. Again, hearing and obeying the Lord's voice are strongly emphasized.

This chapter of the Bible sets forth two different possible outcomes for Israel: first, blessings for obedience, and second, curses for disobedience. In each case, the outcome of either blessings or curses is determined by whether the people obey God's voice.

Here are the first two verses of Deuteronomy 28:

Now it shall come to pass, if you diligently obey the voice of the Lord your God, to observe carefully all His commandments which I command you today, that the Lord your God will set you high above all

nations of the earth. And all these blessings shall
come upon you and overtake you, because you obey
the voice of the Lord your God....

Did you notice how this passage begins and ends
with the idea of diligently listening to the voice of the
Lord? What is the end result of this diligent listening?
"All these blessings shall come upon you and overtake
you."

Next, let's look at the opposite side of the picture,
which is spelled out later in the same chapter:

But it shall come to pass, if you do not obey the voice
of the Lord your God, to observe carefully all His
commandments and His statutes which I command
you today, that all these curses will come upon you
and overtake you...."   (Deuteronomy 28:15)

The implication of Deuteronomy 28 is very clear.
How foolish we would be to neglect this Scripture! The
promises are plain. If we diligently heed the voice of
the Lord, blessings will come upon us. But if we do not
heed the voice of the Lord, curses will come upon us.

Are you able to see that hearing and obeying God's
voice has been His continuing requirement for His people throughout all ages and dispensations? Basically, it is
very simple. God says, "If you want to be My people – if
you want to enjoy My blessings – then diligently heed
My words. Listen to My voice with both of your ears.

But if you fail to listen – if you refuse to listen to Me – then curses, and not blessings, will come upon you."

As I pointed out from my own experience, this principle applies especially in the matter of healing. Remember that Exodus 15 says, "If you diligently heed the voice of the Lord your God...I am the Lord who heals you" (verse 26). Yet this truth applies to all other provisions and blessings of God as well. What is the key? "If you diligently heed the voice of the Lord your God."

THE UNCHANGING MANDATE

Over the years, through the prophets, God reminded the Israelites of this primary requirement, which He had first placed before them through Moses. The prophet Jeremiah succinctly and vividly sums up their mandate in the following passage. God is reprimanding the Israelites for not understanding what He required of them and for not obeying Him:

> *For I did not speak to your fathers, or command them in the day that I brought them out of the land of Egypt, concerning burnt offerings or sacrifices. But this is what I commanded them, saying, "Obey My voice, and I will be your God, and you shall be My people. And walk in all the ways that I have commanded you, that it may be well with you."*
>
> (Jeremiah 7:22–23)

I believe these verses sum up the life of faith as simply and clearly as can ever be stated: "Obey My voice, and I will be your God." This is the Lord's unvarying requirement from age to age and from dispensation to dispensation. The context and circumstances may change, but the mandate remains constant.

Alas, the Israelites did not do what God required. We see this fact clearly from what Jeremiah expresses in the next verse:

> *Yet they did not obey or incline their ear, but followed the counsels and the dictates of their evil hearts, and went backward and not forward.*
>
> (Jeremiah 7:24)

What was the Israelites' great problem? We could cite many outward manifestations of their condition. But the inward essence of the issue is stated in these words: "Yet they did not obey or incline their ear." Please notice that it all revolves around what the Israelites listened to – or did not listen to. They didn't bow down their ear. They didn't listen for the Lord's voice to hear what He wanted them to do. Instead, what did they listen to? Their own hearts, and what their own instincts were telling them to do. As a result, they missed the whole of God's purposes and plans.

Remember that God said in Exodus 19, "If you will indeed obey My voice and keep My covenant, then you shall be a special treasure to Me above all people. . . .

And you shall be to Me a kingdom of priests and a holy nation" (verses 5–6). These verses carry the same message I just cited from Jeremiah 7:23: "Obey My voice, and I will be your God."

I can't emphasize this truth strongly enough. If you really want to belong to the Lord – if you want to walk in His ways and enjoy His blessings – here is what He is saying to you, just as He said to Israel: "Obey My voice, and I will be your God."

SIX

The Mark of Christ's Sheep

We have seen that, in various periods of history, God has dealt with mankind in different ways. In theological language, dispensations is the term used for these different periods of God's dealings with humanity.

Let us briefly recap the three main dispensations. First, the dispensation of the Patriarchs – when God dealt with individuals and their families in a personal relationship. Second, the dispensation of the Law – when God placed the nation of Israel under a special law and dealt with them by way of the temple and the priesthood. Third, the dispensation of the Gospel – the one in which we are living today. The gospel is the universal proclamation from God to all mankind regarding salvation through Jesus Christ, and it requires an individual response from everyone who hears it.

In each of these distinct dispensations, the one common, unvarying requirement for all of God's people has been to hear His voice.

THE GOOD SHEPHERD

In the New Testament, Jesus's teachings carry the same pivotal message we noted in the Old Testament with the examples of Moses and Jeremiah. I want you to see again that with respect to this requirement, nothing has changed. As we discussed, there may have been a change of context and circumstances, but this crucial mandate of hearing and obeying the Lord's voice has remained constant.

In this regard, I want to quote several verses from John 10, where Jesus presents Himself as the Good Shepherd. The following is how Jesus describes the relationship between a true shepherd and his sheep, using this analogy to depict Himself as the Shepherd and His people as the sheep:

> To him [the shepherd] the doorkeeper opens, and the sheep hear his voice; and he calls his own sheep by name and leads them out.   (John 10:3)

What is the mark of Jesus's sheep? They hear the Shepherd's voice.

KNOWING HIS VOICE

John 10:4 adds another important element to the picture:

And when he brings out his own sheep, he goes before them; and the sheep follow him, for they know His voice.

What is the great basis of our relationship with the Lord Jesus? We follow Him. Why? Because we know His voice. The next verse clarifies this point:

Yet they [the sheep] will by no means follow a stranger, but will flee from him, for they do not know the voice of strangers. (John 10:5)

Once again, we see that everything revolves around hearing and knowing the voice of the Lord. God's people recognize His voice, and they follow Him. They will not follow deceivers. They will not follow false prophets and errant teachers. Why? Because they recognize that the voices of these others are not the voice of the Lord. The fact that they know the voice of the Lord enables them to keep from being deceived by the false prophets and teachers.

Up to this point, Jesus has been speaking about believers among the people of Israel. But in John 10:16, He goes on to talk about people from other nations:

I have other sheep, which are not of this fold [not of the Jewish fold]; I must bring them also, and they will hear My voice; and they will become one flock with one shepherd. (NASB)

What draws believers to Jesus from among all Gen-
tile nations? How are they able to come to Him? This
verse provides the answer to these questions: "they will
hear My voice." That is the characteristic mark of all who
come to Jesus and follow Him as their Shepherd.

What Jesus says in this context is very significant for
attaining Christian unity: "They will become one flock
with one shepherd" (John 10:16). What is the way to
achieve unity among believers? I do not believe it will
come primarily through planning and organization. I
do not think it will come mainly through doctrinal or
theological discussions. Unity will come as we all learn
to hear the voice of the Lord. "They will hear My voice,"
Jesus says, "and they will become one flock with one
shepherd" (verse 16).

THREE TRAITS OF FOLLOWERS

Later in John 10, Jesus sums up this principle of hearing
His voice by saying,

> *My sheep hear My voice, and I know them, and they*
> *follow Me.* (John 10:27 NASB)

Three related traits identify true followers of the
Lord: (1) They hear His voice. (2) He knows them –
He recognizes them and acknowledges them. (3) They
follow Him.

Being a follower of Christ is not a question of
belonging to a particular religious group. Jesus is not

talking in terms of Catholics, Protestants, or any specific denominations. Neither is being a follower tied to a certain form of worship or adherence to a particular doctrine. Jesus is not saying, "My people come from one particular group that does things a certain way." But He is saying, "There are characteristic marks that single out My people. These traits distinguish them from all others. They make them different, and they make them Mine. Here are those traits: 'My sheep hear My voice, and I know them, and they follow Me.'"

FOLLOWING HIS VOICE

We must realize that, in biblical times, a shepherd did not drive his sheep. He led them. How did he lead them? By the sound of His voice. The sheep didn't follow mainly by watching him. They followed by listening to Him – and they always went where they heard the shepherd's voice. If we apply this scriptural analogy to our lives, we see that it is impossible to follow the Lord unless we hear and recognize His voice.

As I bring this chapter to a close, let me say something to you in love and sincerity that may be hard to receive. Jesus did not tell us, "My sheep read the Bible." I believe it is essential to read the Bible. But just reading the Word is not sufficient. Many people read the Bible but do not hear the voice of the Lord. It is not reading the Bible that enables us to follow Him. It is hearing His voice, either through His Word or by other spiritual means. As Jesus so clearly stated, "My sheep hear My voice, and I know them, and they follow Me" (John 10:27 NASB).

SEVEN

Three Distinguishing Features

We have clearly established that the ultimate requirement for an ongoing relationship with the Lord – one
that is basic and unchanging – is to hear His voice.
In chapter 5, I pointed out that this requirement is
succinctly summed up in Jeremiah, where God says
through the prophet to His people Israel,

> *Obey My voice, and I will be your God.*
>   (Jeremiah 7:23)

I believe this verse says it all. It represents what God
requires of His people in all ages, all dispensations, all
cultures, and all backgrounds. Many factors in the life
of God's people may change. But this one requirement
never alters. God says, "Do you want Me to be your
God? Then obey My voice."

We have also seen that the foundational requirement Jeremiah stated in the Old Testament is the same requirement Jesus expressed in the New Testament: "My sheep hear My voice, and I know them, and they follow Me" (John 10:27 NASB). This verse describes three steps in the process of following Jesus. It begins with our hearing the voice of Jesus. When we hear His voice, He knows us – He recognizes us, takes note of us, and acknowledges that we are His. Then, we follow Him.

According to the pattern of shepherding in biblical times, the sheep were not driven by the shepherd. They followed him. The sheep followed because they heard the shepherd's voice. If they didn't hear his voice, they couldn't follow him. The same pattern applies to our relationship with Jesus. If we do not hear His voice, we cannot follow Him. We have to hear His voice before we can follow. That is what makes us His sheep.

THREE FEATURES OF HEARING

We will now look at three distinguishing features of hearing God's voice – features that are significantly different from much of what is traditionally accepted as typical religious conduct or activity. Thus, in many ways, this message is revolutionary. It may sound simple, but when we really take it to heart and begin to apply it, we will find that it will change our standards. It will change our values. It will change the way we live.

Here are the three features of hearing God's voice that merit our consideration:

1. Hearing God's voice is personal.
2. Hearing God's voice is intangible.
3. Hearing God's voice is in the present. It is not in the past. It is not in the future. It is always present.

I want you to fully grasp these three features as I take some time to expand upon their meaning.

1. HEARING GOD'S VOICE IS PERSONAL

Hearing God's voice is very personal. Why? No two voices are exactly alike; every voice is individual. In fact, the voice is one of the most distinctive features of the human personality. That is why Jesus was able to say, "[My sheep] will by no means follow a stranger, but will flee from him, for they do not know the voice of strangers" (John 10:5).

You see, our protection in hearing the Lord's voice is relating to Him individually and personally. We are not just relating to a historical figure. We are not just relating to some movement or doctrine. Rather, we are connecting with the Lord Himself through His voice. This involves a direct, intimate, person-to-person relationship with Him.

ℬ ACCESS TO OUR HEART

In the world around us, people are increasingly using

devices that are voice-activated. I have heard of such devices being used as a security measure for the main safe in commercial banks. The only code for the main safe is a specific voice – possibly that of the bank president or manager. No other voice can cause that safe to open. This is an indication of how absolutely distinctive one person's voice is.

To me, the use of these devices in banks is a parable about how we should safeguard our hearts. A bank safe represents what the heart of every believer should be like. Our hearts must guard the most valuable treasure we have. Furthermore, only one voice should be able to open up our "safe" – the voice of the Lord Himself. We will come into terrible grief and problems if we open the door of our heart to the wrong characters. A number of the tragedies and problems in the world today could well be traced to people giving unscrupulous individuals access to their hearts. Many people have learned by experience that when they open their hearts to the wrong individuals or the wrong voices, serious troubles and problems can result.

SPIRITUAL VOICE-ACTIVATION

From now on, I would recommend that you think of your heart as a safe that is voice-activated. Let your heart respond primarily to the voice of the Lord. When you open up your heart to the Lord, you will never be harmed, you will never be deceived, and you will never be disappointed.

The "voice-activation" I have just described is the basis of the Shepherd/sheep relationship. In Psalm 23, David discusses one of the main benefits of this relationship:

The Lord is my shepherd, I lack nothing.

(verse 1 NIV)

On the basis of his personal relationship with the Lord, David was assured that his every need would be supplied. How can the Lord be our Shepherd? Only if we hear His voice. Remember, Jesus said, "My sheep hear My voice" (John 10:27 NASB). If we hear His voice, affirming that He is our Shepherd, then all our needs will be met. Isn't that beautiful? This is one of the primary reasons we need to cultivate our ability to hear the Lord's voice.

2. HEARING GOD'S VOICE IS INTANGIBLE

Second, hearing the Lord's voice is an intangible process. We cannot apprehend it with our sight, touch it with our hands, or even grasp it through our feelings. There is only one sense that perceives a voice. What is it? The sense of hearing.

Many of our religious activities are associated with something tangible. When we think about religion, we

often picture objects in space and time: a church building, a pulpit, an organ, stained-glass windows, prayer
books, hymnals, and special garments for the clergy.

In contrast, hearing God's voice has no tangible
features, and it is not restricted to a particular place. It
does not necessitate visiting a specific building filled
with odd-looking furniture or wearing a certain type
of clothing. In a way, it is very tricky because we have
nothing physical to cling on to. If we truly want to hear
God's voice, we must leave behind all the old religious
associations that we may have looked to for help in the
past – all the "crutches," as Martin Luther called them.
With all the tangibles stripped away, we are left only
with an intimate, personal relationship with the Lord –
an intangible relationship.

3. HEARING GOD'S VOICE
IS IN THE PRESENT

The third feature I wish to point out about hearing God's
voice is that it is always present, in the sense of time.
Hearing God's voice is never in the past and never in
the future. It is always now.

Only in the now can we directly hear a voice. We can
pick up a book, read it, put it down, and say, "I'll look
at it again tomorrow." But a voice is heard only in the
moment. A voice has no past. A voice has no future. It
engages us in the present.

Thus, when we relate to God through hearing His

voice, we are responding to Him in the eternal now. God always is. There is a certain sense in which God is in the past and in the future. But, essentially, we always know God in the eternal present, and His voice is always in the present.

Unfortunately, what I have noticed about religious people is that much of their thinking is about the past or the future. Christians often talk about what happened in the days of Moses, or in the days of Jesus, or in the days of Peter. That is all in the past. Or their focus is on how beautiful it will be when they get to heaven.

Even though I agree with their sentiments, we are not living in the past, and we are not living in the future. We are living in the present. Because they mainly focus on the past or the future, many religious people hardly live at all. But when we realize that we have to relate to God through hearing His voice, it forces us into a present relationship and a present experience with Him.

✎ "I AM HAS SENT ME"

It is interesting to note that when God appeared to Moses in the midst of the burning bush and sent him back to deliver His people from Egypt, Moses asked a very practical question. The Lord answered this question with a profound revelation:

> Moses said to God, "Suppose I go to the Israelites and say to them, 'The God of your fathers has sent

me to you,' and they ask me, 'What is His name?'
Then what shall I tell them?" God said to Moses,
"I am who I am. This is what you are to say to the
Israelites: 'I am has sent me to you.'"

(Exodus 3:13–14 NIV)

I am is present. It is not past or future. God's name is present. God is living now. Our relationship with Him needs to be now. When we learn to hear the Lord's voice, we can enjoy a present, personal relationship with Him.

As you've been reading about our need for such a relationship with God, perhaps you've realized that you've slipped from that position. You may have to admit that it has been a long time since you've heard the Lord speak to you.

Maybe this would be a good point to renew that connection, asking the Lord to let you hear His voice again. Would you like to do that? I invite you to pray the following prayer:

Dear Lord, I want to hear Your voice again. I long
for You to speak to me – guiding me, comforting
me, and directing my life. I want my heart to open
only to the sound of Your voice. Would You make
that happen once again, Lord? I ask that You would
speak to me – and I open my heart and my ears to
hear Your voice anew. Amen.

EIGHT

Hearing God's Voice Produces Faith

We turn now to a particular result of hearing God's voice that is of inestimable value to us: faith. There is no way we can adequately express the importance of this result.

THE SECRET TO FAITH

Many people long for faith, so they struggle to obtain it, running to and fro as they seek it out. However, they have not been successful using this approach. Why not? Because they have not discovered the secret of faith, which is this: faith comes by hearing God's voice. This principle is stated in the book of Romans:

> *So faith comes from hearing, and hearing by [or from] the word of Christ.* (Romans 10:17 NASB)

To understand this principle, we need to recognize that in New Testament Greek, there are two different terms that can be translated into English as "word": logos and rhema. It is essential for you to know the difference between them.

Otherwise, it will be difficult to grasp the meaning of what we cover in this chapter.

THE WORD AS *LOGOS*

Let's look at the word logos first. Logos is one of the great concepts of the Greek language. I have been studying Greek since I was ten years old, and I know Greek well enough to be qualified to teach it at the university level. I say this only to make it clear that I have some idea of what I am talking about. Logos has all sorts of meanings. It is a comprehensive word, among whose definitions are "mind," "counsel," or "reason."

As used in the Bible, logos refers to the mind of God or the counsel of God. It signifies His total purpose. For example, this is what David says about God's Word in Psalm 119:89 (the original term for "word" in Hebrew is dabar, which corresponds with the Greek word logos):

Forever, O Lord, Your word is settled in heaven.

(NASB)

The New International Version translates this verse as follows:

Your word, Lord, is eternal; it stands firm in the heavens.

God's Word is eternal. It is outside of time. It is in heaven. It is settled. It never changes. From beginning to end, it is always there, all the time. Logos represents the mind, the counsel, and the purpose of God.

LOGOS PERSONIFIED

The Bible tells us that this logos – this counsel of God – is summed up in a Person. John 1:1–2 says,

In the beginning was the Word [logos], and the Word was with God, and the Word was God. He was in the beginning with God. (NASB)

Jesus is the personified logos. He is the embodiment of God's total mind, counsel, and purpose. Recall these words of Jesus: "He who has seen Me has seen the Father" (John 14:9). Jesus was saying that He represents everything the Father is, everything the Father does, and everything the Father purposes, wills, and plans.

So, let's remember that logos is settled forever in heaven. It can't be changed because it is eternal.

THE WORD AS *RHEMA*

Rhema has a different meaning than logos, although the connotations of these words can overlap at times. The term rhema specifically refers to a spoken word. It is not a rhema unless it is spoken. God's Word, God's counsel, is forever settled in heaven – whether it is spoken or not. It is there, and it is eternal. But a rhema is a word of God that is spoken.

I am not saying we necessarily hear this word audibly. It may come to us through the Scriptures or even through something another person says to us. God often speaks to us in our spirit, and we learn to recognize when He is specifically communicating with us.

Please note what Jesus says using the word rhema in Matthew 4:

> It is written, "Man shall not live on bread alone, but on every word [rhema] that proceeds out of the mouth of God."   (Matthew 4:4 NASB)

Jesus is speaking about every rhema that proceeds from the mouth of God. Every proceeding word. If you can picture it, the counsel of God is in heaven – eternal, unchanged, complete. As humans, we don't know the entire counsel of God. Our finite minds are not able to comprehend His whole counsel. So, what does God do? He measures out a portion of that counsel to us in a rhema – in a word that is spoken to us. This word becomes personal for us when we receive it.

NOT BY BREAD ALONE

We live by every word that proceeds from the mouth

of God. The total counsel of God is imparted to us in portions, as we are able to receive it – rhema by rhema by rhema. The implication is that God has a rhema for us each day. Jesus says, in essence, "Man shall not live by bread alone; rather, every day, man lives by the proceeding word of God." The word of God – the rhema that comes from the mouth of God – will be our portion for that day.

To summarize the difference between logos and rhema, logos is the unchanging, eternal counsel of God in heaven, while rhema is a personal word that God speaks to us. Let's keep these definitions in mind as we look again at Romans 10:17: "So faith comes from hearing, and hearing by the word of Christ" (NASB). The term translated "word" here is rhema. Faith comes from hearing the rhema – the spoken word of Christ. If it weren't spoken, we couldn't hear it. We can't hear the logos; that is the eternal counsel of God in heaven. But we are able to hear the rhema, which brings us the portion of God's counsel we need at a given moment. It comes to us personally. And that is how faith comes.

HOW FAITH *DOESN'T* COME

Notice that Romans 10:17 doesn't say that faith comes from reading the Bible. Lots of people think it does. You may ask, "Why not?" To be honest, as I said previously, we can read the Bible but hear nothing! At such times, all we have in front of our eyes is black marks on white paper. We might read the Bible for an hour and yet not receive any faith.

At other times, we might simply pick up the Bible, open it, and have one sentence leap out of the page at us. When we see it, we exclaim, "That's it! That is what God is saying to me." I can't count how many times this has happened in my life. Sometimes, quite unexpectedly, when I open the Bible, the Holy Spirit focuses my eyes on a verse. As I read the verse, God says, "This is My rhema for you right now."

When you hear that rhema, there is more happening than just your reading the Bible. God is communicating a personal word to you. Receiving that word first requires His voice speaking to you. Faith comes by hearing the spoken word of God.

Can you see how faith is dependent on rhema? It all centers around hearing God's voice. This principle corresponds to the following verses, which we studied earlier: "Obey My voice, and I will be your God" (Jeremiah 7:23), and "If you diligently heed the voice of the Lord your God..., I will put none of the diseases on you which I have brought on the Egyptians" (Exodus 15:26). It is all part of the same process of hearing God's voice.

HOW FAITH COMES

Let's look once more at Romans 10:17:

So faith comes from hearing, and hearing by the word [rhema] of Christ. (NASB)

To help explain how faith "comes," I would like to give you an example from what I have learned and experienced in my own life. I believe that what I share will be of incalculable value to you if you can grasp it.

As I mentioned previously, when I was a young man, I suffered with an illness for which the doctors could find no cure. This was during my military service, shortly after I became a Christian, and I was in the hospital for a whole year. Because the doctors were unable to heal me, I realized that my only hope was in God. As time went on, I found myself saying, "If I had faith, I know God would heal me." Then, I would always say, "But I don't have faith."

This went on for quite a while until, one day, as I was reading my Bible, a rhema came to me from Romans 10:17: "Faith cometh by hearing" (KJV). I leapt at that phrase, "Faith cometh." Here is what I realized: if I don't have faith, I can get it! After looking at the rest of the verse, I pondered, I prayed, and I sought God. Gradually, the Lord opened up the meaning of this Scripture to me. Once He had opened up that meaning – how faith comes – I was able to receive the faith I needed for my healing.

I thank God for the ministry of doctors and nurses, but in that instance, they weren't able to heal me. My healing had to come directly from the Lord. When and how did that healing come? Only after I had heard the rhema, the spoken word of God, which brought faith to me.

So, there is a process by which faith comes, and if you can take hold of this process, it will change your life. As I have learned, there are three stages to this process:

1. You look for God's rhema in His Word, asking for His guidance.
2. You respond. You open yourself to the Word of God. This means that you are in a posture of wanting to hear what God says to you.
3. Out of your hearing, faith comes. Often, there is an element of time in the hearing stage. Hearing doesn't usually happen instantaneously. Sometimes, it can come in a moment, but it often takes place over a period of time.

THE RIGHT ATTITUDE

For faith to come, we have to position ourselves with a certain attitude or frame of mind. We can be reading the Bible or listening to a sermon, but the words simply fly right past us. To hear God's voice, it is necessary for us to settle down into a kind of inner stillness – a condition in which our mind is at rest and our usually busy mental processes are suspended for a moment.

This is the point where we are hearing. And it is out of that hearing that faith comes.

I strongly encourage you to cultivate this ability to hear. Be open to what God is saying to you personally. Remember that a rhema word will always be in line with the Scriptures; it will never contradict the Word of God. You will find that God's rhema to you will be Scripture-quickened – made alive and personal by the Holy Spirit.

That is how faith comes – by hearing the voice of God.

PART III
Led by the Spirit

NINE
A Distinctive Lifestyle

In the previous chapter, we discussed a specific result of hearing God's voice that is of inestimable value. What is that outcome? Faith. This is a result that, if nothing else ever followed, would make it well worth our while to hear God's voice.

We also talked about how there are two Greek terms translated as "word" in the New Testament. The first is logos – the divine, eternal, unchanging counsel of God that is settled forever in heaven. We recognized that our finite human minds cannot fully understand logos. The second word, rhema, is part of the solution for our limited comprehension of God's mind and counsel. A rhema is a word that God speaks to us individually, one that has been quickened by the Holy Spirit. Rhema brings to us the aspect of God's counsel that we need at a given moment. When the Lord sends us a rhema word, He makes it vivid and personal to us.

Faith comes to us by hearing this personal, spoken word of God. It may come to us through the Scriptures or even through something another person says to us. But it always comes by the leading of the Holy Spirit.

PEOPLE WHO HEAR

We will now examine the distinctive lifestyle that results from hearing the voice of God. People who learn to hear God's voice lead a life that is different from other people. They simply can't be the same after hearing the Lord's mind and counsel.

We will begin by returning to a Scripture that I quoted in the previous chapter. This verse is Jesus's answer to Satan during their wilderness confrontation when the devil tempted Him to turn stones into bread:

> It is written, "Man shall not live on bread alone,
> but on every word that proceeds out of the mouth
> of God." (Matthew 4:4 NASB)

The Greek term rendered "word" is rhema – "every rhema that proceeds out of the mouth of God." The verb "proceeds" is in the continuing present tense, expressing the idea of "every proceeding word," or every word as it proceeds from the mouth of God. This meaning shows us why hearing God's voice involves a direct personal relationship with the Lord.

The "proceeding" characteristic of a rhema word

means that, in the instant it comes, we are in tune with God – right then, right there. Rhema is not past, and it is not future. It is in the present, the here and now. The word we receive is the continuing, proceeding word of God for that given moment, for that given time, for that given situation. This is the kind of word that we live on!

THE BREAD WE NEED

In Matthew 4:4, Jesus quoted Deuteronomy 8:3, which refers to God providing the Israelites with manna in the wilderness. In a certain sense, by drawing on this analogy, Jesus was comparing rhema with natural bread. In the same way natural bread feeds our physical body, this proceeding, personal word of God feeds our spirit. It nourishes our inner being. We must recognize the fact that we need one type of bread just as much as we need the other. To keep our bodies alive and healthy, we need natural bread. To keep our spirits alive and healthy, we need spiritual bread – the proceeding word, the personal word from God. We need to hear the voice of the Lord as it comes to us.

RELYING ON THE HOLY SPIRIT

This word that we need for feeding our spirit comes only through the Holy Spirit – and we must hear it. Again, if we merely hold a Bible in front of us, all we have is white sheets of paper with black marks on them. We can't hear those marks. That is impossible. How can they ever become a voice – a spoken communication that we can hear? Only one power in the universe can turn those black marks into the voice of God – and that power is the Holy Spirit.

At the beginning of this book, I talked about how important it is that we, as the body of Christ, remain connected to the Head. We saw that it is the Holy Spirit through whom Jesus communicates, directs, controls, and preserves His body. Can you see how this revelation of rhema ties in with those truths?

We are totally dependent on the Holy Spirit. The Spirit is the One who brings the rhema word to us in any given situation. He brings us the word from God we need right now. The Holy Spirit quickens that word, imparting life to it, making it a living voice for us to hear. Through hearing God's word, we connect strongly with the Head, our Lord Jesus, through the Holy Spirit. The Spirit guides and directs us all the way through that process – every moment of every day – by the rhemas He gives us.

TEN

Sons and Daughters of God

Having a life marked by hearing the voice of God makes us different from most others around us. Developing this lifestyle is a growing, deepening process in our lives – one that we would do well to understand fully. Please note what Paul says about this process in Romans 8:14:

> *For all who are being led by the Spirit of God, these are sons of God.* (NASB)

The Greek word translated "son" in this verse does not refer to a child but to an adult. How are we to live as adult children of God? There is only one way: by being regularly led by His Spirit. Just as we saw in Matthew 4:4 in relation to the word "proceeds," the Greek word for "led" in Romans 8:14 is in the continuing present tense. The meaning of this verse in Romans is clear. It refers to people who are regularly or continually led by the Spirit of God. It is such individuals who are known as the sons and daughters of God.

AN ONGOING RELATIONSHIP

Sadly, some of the people who talk the most about the Holy Spirit know the least about being led by Him. I have been connected to the Pentecostal denomination for many decades. I am not ashamed of my Pentecostal roots. In fact, I thank God for Pentecostals because I owe my salvation to them. Even so, it is troubling to me to hear some people say, in essence, "I was baptized in the Holy Spirit fifteen years ago, and I spoke in tongues, and that's all I need." Some of these people are actually far out of touch with the Holy Spirit today. Encountering the Holy Spirit is not a one-time experience. It is an ongoing relationship.

Ephesians 2:18–22 has much to say concerning our relationship with the Spirit. We will look at two verses from this passage, beginning with verse 18:

For through Him [Jesus] we both [Jews and Gentiles] have access by one Spirit to the Father.

May I point out that this verse mentions all three persons of the Godhead? Through Jesus, by the Spirit, to the Father. That is a healthy pattern for our interaction with the Lord.

Next, verse 22 gives us this description of believers:

In whom [Jesus] you also are being built together for a dwelling place ["habitation" KJV] of God in the Spirit.

Simply put, by the Spirit, God indwells those who are in Jesus. In both aspects and directions of that interaction – upward and downward – the link is the Holy Spirit. If you miss out on the Holy Spirit, there is no connection. You can have all sorts of good doctrine and religious activity, but if the Holy Spirit isn't there, you have no contact with God. The Spirit is the only way by which you can access the Father.

Thus, what makes us God's sons and daughters? Being led by His Spirit.

LED BY THE SPIRIT

There are many different ways in which the Holy Spirit works in our lives. Let us examine two of those ways. First, we are born again of the Holy Spirit, becoming newborn children – babies – in Christ. In his first epistle, Peter said, "As newborn babes, desire the pure milk of the word" (1 Peter 2:2). We start as newborns, desiring the milk of God's Word. Yet, desiring the Word, in itself, doesn't make us mature sons and daughters of God. We become mature only by being led by the Holy Spirit.

All who are being led by the Spirit of God are sons

and daughters of God. They are not babies, not children, but mature grown-ups. Please note again that this aspect of being led by the Spirit is a continuing, ongoing, present reality – all who are being continually led by God's Spirit. This is not something that just happens once. Neither is it something we experience once a week at a church service. It is going on all the time in our daily lives. It is our "daily bread." We are led as we hear the voice of the Lord through the Holy Spirit. As we hear His voice, we receive direction for our lives.

THE "ORGANIZER"

Whenever my wife and I plan our day or go about our normal routines, we pray a specific prayer. This is the same prayer I mentioned near the beginning of this book – that we may always be in the right place at the right time. We have discovered that praying in this fashion makes a big difference! The right outcomes seem to occur in our lives.

We spend a good deal of our time in Jerusalem, and in that city, the means of communication are limited. A lot of people don't have phones. Few people have cars. The mail system is rather ineffective. (We once posted a letter from one address in Jerusalem to another, and it took seventeen days to arrive.) So, how are we able to communicate with people?

One of our solutions to this challenge is to pray this prayer to always be in the right place at the right time.

Afterward, it is amazing how often, without planning it, we come in contact with the very person we need to meet at the very moment we need to speak with them. Who organizes that? The Holy Spirit. He is the One who leads us. For instance, He may tell us, "Today is the day to go to the bank." When we go to the bank, we see someone we need to contact standing in front of us in the line for the cashier. Or, the Spirit's communication will be, "Don't catch that bus; take another one." When we take the different bus, we meet up with the people we needed to see. These are examples of rhema. It is the spoken word by which we receive the ongoing direction of the Holy Spirit.

Our seasoned ability to hear the rhema word in this way is what makes us mature sons and daughters of God. The first step, of course, is to be born again by God's Spirit. We start as little babies. Then, we become grown-ups by learning to regularly hear the voice of the Lord.

MOMENT BY MOMENT

I now want to show you that this lifestyle I am describing – receiving God's word as our daily bread, having the Holy Spirit speak to us personally – was the lifestyle of Jesus Himself.

Christ not only preached this way of life, but He also practiced it.

In Isaiah 50:4–7, there is a beautiful, prophetic picture of the earthly life of our Lord. It describes His ministry and His ongoing, daily relationship with God the Father. Jesus is the speaker in this passage, which begins,

> *The sovereign Lord has given Me an instructed*
> *tongue, to know the word that sustains the weary.*
>   (Isaiah 50:4 NIV84)

We know that Jesus was able to speak a word that would sustain the weary. How was that made possible?

> *He [the Father] wakens Me morning by morning,*
> *wakens My ear to listen like one being taught.*
>   (verse 4 NIV84)

That was Jesus's secret. God awakened His ear every morning. He heard His Father's voice speaking to Him, guiding Him, and giving Him instruction and strength for the day. We read more about this process in Isaiah 4:5:

> *The Sovereign Lord has opened my ears, and I*
> *have not been rebellious; I have not drawn back.*
>   (NIV84)

In the next verse, we have a very clear, prophetic picture of Jesus in His suffering:

> *I offered My back to those who beat Me, My cheeks*
> *to those who pulled out My beard; I did not hide*
> *My face from mocking and spitting.*
>   (Isaiah 50:6 NIV)

Why was Jesus willing to go through all that He endured? How did He receive the strength for it? Here is the answer: by hearing the Father's voice. Every morning, Jesus heard from His Father before He communicated with human beings.

Isaiah 50:7 goes on to speak about the outcome of this kind of mature relationship with the Father:

Because the Sovereign Lord helps Me, I will not be disgraced. Therefore have I set My face like flint, and I know I will not be put to shame. (NIV)

EFFECTS OF HEARING THE FATHER'S VOICE

From this passage in Isaiah, let's summarize what Jesus experienced as a result of listening to the Father each day:

- He had words of encouragement for others.
- He received personal direction for Himself.
- He achieved obedience. We need to see that hearing and executing God's voice produces obedience.
- He received strength to go through all that He had to endure. He needed more than human strength; He needed supernatural empowerment. How did He receive it? Through hearing the Father's voice.
- He received determination. In His obedience, Jesus said, "I've set My face like flint; I'm not turning back."

Jesus obtained all of these results through hearing the Father's voice. Even more amazing for us is this truth: through hearing the Holy Spirit's voice, we will receive the same results Jesus received! When we cultivate the habit of letting the Lord awaken our ear each morning, we will experience what Jesus experienced. When we start each day hearing the voice of the Father, we will walk as sons and daughters of God who are led by His Spirit.

Let me ask you this: is it your desire to live every day being led by the Holy Spirit and to experience the same results Jesus experienced? If your answer is yes, would you pray with me now to express that desire to the Lord?

Lord, I want to live my life hearing Your voice each step of the way. Will You "waken my ear" every morning? Will You allow me to hear Your voice and then help me to obey what You tell me?

This is my prayer, Lord. Please grant it by the power of the Holy Spirit and in the name of Jesus. Amen.

ELEVEN

Hearing from the Heart

We know that the great, unchanging, basic requirement for an ongoing relationship with God is to hear His voice. In the Old Testament, the Lord summed up this fact in one brief statement, conveyed by the prophet Jeremiah:

> *Obey My voice, and I will be your God.*
>
> (Jeremiah 7:23)

In all ages and dispensations, God says, "The one response that ultimately matters is to obey My voice. Then, I will be your God."

FOLLOWING JESUS

In the New Testament, Jesus states the one identifying mark of all those, in every age, who would truly be His disciples:

*My sheep hear My voice, and I know them, and they
follow Me.* (John 10:27 NASB)

What Jesus describes here is not a denominational
label. It is not a particular doctrinal emphasis. Rather,
He depicts those who hear His voice and follow Him.
Hearing Jesus's voice is essential to being one of His
followers.

In chapter 8, I explained that true faith comes as the
result of hearing God's voice:

*So faith comes from hearing, and hearing by the
word of Christ.* (Romans 10:17 NASB)

As we cultivate the practice of hearing God's personal word to us each day, it becomes the fresh, daily
bread that nourishes us spiritually. Through this practice, we receive daily direction and strength for our
ongoing walk with God.

EARS TO HEAR

In the chapters that follow, I discuss the practical out-
working of hearing God's voice. We will explore and
answer the question, "How can we hear God's voice?"

To begin, let's turn to Jesus's teachings in the Gos-
pels. Many times, He talked about people needing "ears
to hear," particularly when He was speaking in parables.
For instance, in the gospel of Mark, after Jesus gave the
parable of the sower, He said,

He who has ears to hear, let him hear!

(Mark 4:9)

A little further on in the same chapter, Jesus says,

If anyone has ears to hear, let him hear.

(Mark 4:23)

What does it mean to have "ears to hear"? Obviously, Jesus was not referring to physical ears and natural hearing. Presumably, all the people who were listening to His teachings were in possession of two physical ears – at least, the great majority of them were. And most of those in His audience were not physically deaf.

Even so, Jesus said, "If anyone has ears to hear, let him hear." What was He talking about? I am of the opinion that He was referring to an inner condition of the heart. I believe the essence of what Jesus was saying is that we have to hear God with our heart. How is it possible for us to have a heart to hear God – a hearing heart?

"GIVE YOUR SERVANT A DISCERNING HEART"

To help answer this question, let us now turn to an example from the life of Solomon. Early in Solomon's reign as king of Israel, the Lord appeared to him in a dream and asked him a vital question – "What do you want?" – in the form of a statement:

At Gibeon the Lord appeared to Solomon during the night in a dream, and God said, "Ask for whatever you want Me to give you." (1 Kings 3:5 NIV)

I am not sure that I would be ready to face that type of situation. Imagine if God appeared to you and said, "Ask Me for what you want, and I will give it to you." What would you ask for? Would you respond in the same way Solomon did? Here is how Solomon answered the Lord:

Now, Lord my God, you have made your servant king in place of my father David. But I am only a little child and do not know how to carry out my duties. Your servant is here among the people you have chosen, a great people, too numerous to count or number. (1 Kings 3:7–8 NIV)

When Solomon was confronted with a situation that was much too big for him, he realized he couldn't handle it on his own. In such a circumstance, what should he ask for? This is how he responded:

So give your servant a discerning heart to govern your people and to distinguish between right and wrong. For who is able to govern this great people of yours? (1 Kings 3:9 NIV)

After recording Solomon's reply, the biblical writer comments,

*The Lord was pleased that Solomon had asked for
this.*   (verse 10 NIV)

In verse 9, where the New International Version
renders the phrase "a discerning heart," the original
Hebrew literally says, "a hearing heart." That quality
is what we have been specifically talking about in this
chapter – and, indeed, in this entire book. We need
a heart that can hear God. As a result of his request,
Solomon received what he had asked for as a gift from
God. God gave him a discerning, hearing heart simply
because he had requested it.

Let me pause here in our discussion to inquire,
"Have you ever asked God for a hearing heart?" We
know that it is with our heart – not usually with our
physical ears – that we hear the voice of God. Do you
realize that it will make all the difference in your life
whether you can hear God's voice with your heart?

A GUARDED HEART

In a previous chapter, to illustrate how we need to guard
our hearts, I used the example of a bank safe. Our heart
is the place where we keep our treasure, what really matters to us. In the example, the bank safe is programmed
electronically to open only at the voice of the bank manager. The manager's voice, like every voice, is unique.
There is no way to copy it. So, the only one who can
open the safe is that manager, when he speaks certain

words with his voice. Similarly, only the voice of the Lord should be able to open our hearts to receive His eternal purpose and direction for our lives.

The following words of Solomon remind us of this truth:

> *Keep your heart with all diligence, for out of it spring the issues of life.* (Proverbs 4:23)

What you have stored in your heart will settle the course of your life. Your heart is a safe that holds treasures much more precious than those kept in a bank safe. Personally, I believe every child of God should have a heart like a safe – one that is programmed to open only for the voice of the Lord.

Remember that Jesus said, "My sheep hear My voice, and I know them, and they follow Me" (John 10:27 NASB). His sheep will not follow a stranger because they do not recognize the stranger's voice. How important it is to have a heart that will only open to the voice of the Lord – not to an alien or a stranger! What kind of heart does God want us to have? A hearing heart. In our spirit, we have ears to hear. In the innermost depths of our being, we have a heart that responds to the voice of the Lord.

SPIRITUAL DEAFNESS

If we want to have a hearing heart, it is crucial for us to

avoid the opposite condition, which is spiritual deafness. In both the Old and New Testaments, the Bible has much to say about people's inability to hear God's voice. Jesus indicated that those who could not understand His parables were spiritually deaf. In the gospel of Matthew, He expressed it in this way:

> *This is why I speak to them in parables: "Though seeing, they do not see; though hearing, they do not hear or understand. In them is fulfilled the prophecy of Isaiah: 'You will be ever hearing but never understanding; you will be ever seeing but never perceiving. For this people's heart has become calloused; they hardly hear with their ears, and they have closed their eyes. Otherwise, they might see with their eyes, hear with their ears, understand with their hearts and turn, and I would heal them.'"*
>
> (Matthew 13:13–15 NIV)

Jesus gives us a picture of people who have no heart to hear the voice of the Lord. They have become inwardly deaf. In this depiction, Jesus uses a very significant word, which is also very frightening: "This people's heart has become calloused." What is He saying? Their heart doesn't respond to God anymore. It is no longer sensitive.

We see a similar idea in this Old Testament admonition to the Israelites from Psalm 95:

Today, if you hear His voice, do not harden your hearts as you did at Meribah, as you did that day at Massah in the desert. (verses 7–8 NIV84)

God says the following about those who did harden their hearts:

For forty years I was angry with that generation; I said, "They are a people whose hearts go astray, and they have not known My ways." So I declared on oath in My anger, "They shall never enter My rest." (verses 10–11 NIV)

I believe that a number of God's people today never really enter into the Lord's rest. They always seem to be wandering in the wilderness, outside of the promised land. What is the reason for this? Could it be that they haven't learned to hear God's voice? The only way to enter God's rest is to hear His voice.

CULTIVATING SENSITIVITY

In the previous examples of spiritual deafness – one from the New Testament and one from the Old Testament – we noted two significant words that describe such a condition of the heart: calloused and hardened. Hearts with these characteristics do not hear. What is the opposite of being calloused and hardened? I would say the significant word is sensitive. We have to cultivate inward sensitivity toward the Lord and His voice.

Let me give you a picture of the type of sensitivity that is needed. Have you ever seen a blind person reading braille? Have you seen their fingers skimming over those little dots on paper? If I were to brush my fingers over those dots, they would mean nothing to me. I would simply feel little bumps on the surface of the paper. But to blind people who have sensitized their fingers, those dots convey meaning. They are words. They carry a message.

I believe that is what it means to cultivate a sensitive heart toward the voice of the Lord. It is to have our hearts so attuned to Him that when He speaks, we hear His voice. And it means something to us. This is one of the real keys to receiving God's ongoing blessings and entering into our inheritance in Him.

When I think of the people mentioned in Psalm 95 who wandered in the wilderness for years, it grieves me tremendously. The Israelites could have been in the promised land earlier if they had only cultivated a sensitive heart toward the voice of the Lord. May I challenge you to do what the Israelites did not do? May I plead with you to cultivate a sensitive heart toward the Lord?

A PLIABLE HEART

I want to provide you with another opportunity to respond to the Holy Spirit's work in your life. As you have been reading this book, perhaps you have sensed the Spirit stirring your heart. Maybe He has been reminding you of times when He spoke to you, but you didn't follow through with what He asked you to do. If what I'm saying hits home, will you take a moment now to repent? Let's say the following prayer together to assist in that process:

Father, thank You for Your Word and Your Spirit, which quicken my heart to hear Your voice. Thank You for Your great love for me. Thank You for chastening me because You love me.

I ask You to forgive me for the many times when I have been presumptuous in taking the initiative to run my own life. Please help me to cultivate a soft and sensitive heart that is able to hear Your voice, and give me the courage to live the life You are leading me to live. I ask You to give me a "hearing heart," as You gave to Solomon, so that I can be completely focused as I listen to You. In Jesus's name, I pray. Amen.

TWELVE

Requirements for Hearing

In my own personal walk with God, I can think of no factor that is more important than learning to hear His voice – and hearing it correctly. Hearing God's voice correctly is usually the key factor in achieving true spiritual success.

GOD DOESN'T SHOUT

In the previous chapter, we saw that people fail to hear God's voice when their hearts are calloused and hardened. This means that in order to hear His voice, we must cultivate sensitivity in our hearts in much the same way that a blind person reading braille cultivates sensitivity in their fingers.

We were also challenged by Solomon's prayer, "Give me a hearing heart." We saw that the Lord was pleased with that request. I asked you a question then, and I will ask it of you again here: have you ever asked God for a hearing heart? If not, won't you begin to do so today?

As we develop sensitivity, we need to understand this characteristic of God: He doesn't shout. Many people picture God as a big man shouting with a loud voice. But that is not God at all. Rarely in Scripture do we see evidence of the Lord shouting. As a matter of fact, later in this book, we will look at an example in which God spoke in a whisper.

SIX REQUIREMENTS FOR DEVELOPING SENSITIVITY

Let us now review six specific requirements for achieving the kind of sensitivity of heart that can hear God's voice – even when He speaks in a whisper.

✎ ATTENTION AND HUMILITY

The first two requirements are closely connected. I summarize them as attention and humility. In the book of Proverbs, these requirements are mentioned many times. Bear in mind that Proverbs was written by King Solomon, the man who had asked God for a hearing heart.

We will look at three verses where these two requirements are joined together. I have capitalized the pronouns related to the speaker to apply these verses to our relationship with God. The first is Proverbs 4:20:

*My son, give attention to My words; incline your
ear to My sayings.*

The two instructions here are to "give attention"
and "incline your ear." To incline your ear means to
bow your head. Bowing your head is a mark of reverent,
respectful humility. You are not arguing with God. You
are not dictating to God. You are waiting to hear from
Him. Inclining your ear is an essential part of hearing
from God.

We see this idea again in the next reference, which
is Proverbs 5:1:

*My son, pay attention to My wisdom; lend your ear
to My understanding.*

In the King James Version, "lend your ear" is rendered as "bow thine ear." So, in this verse, we find the
same two conditions expressed in only slightly different
language: "pay attention" and "lend [bow] your ear."

The final reference is Proverbs 22:17:

*Incline your ear and hear the words of the wise, and
apply your heart to My knowledge.*

The first part of this verse, "Incline your ear and hear
the words of the wise," has a clear implication: basically,
if we don't bow down our ear, we won't be able to hear.
If we don't have the right attitude toward God – an
attitude of humility, respectfulness, and reverence – we

will not hear. The verse concludes with, "Apply your heart to My knowledge." All of the verses I have cited emphasize the same overall truth: it is the heart that hears the voice of God. We have to apply our heart to hearing. We have to focus our attention on hearing.

❧ OUR UNDIVIDED ATTENTION

Let's sum up these requirements for hearing God's voice. First, we must give the Lord our undivided attention, applying our heart to hear Him. In many ways, this concept is totally contrary to contemporary culture, where most people are used to listening to at least two different sounds or sources of information at the same time.

When one of my daughters was still in high school, I saw her sitting at our kitchen counter doing her homework while watching a television program. Frankly, my mind reeled. I have been a student, a teacher, and a university professor – and I absolutely could never do that. If I were watching television, I could not focus on my homework. If I were focusing on my homework, I could not intelligently watch television. Now, I am not saying that my daughter didn't achieve any results. But I am sure she didn't achieve the maximum results that she would have if she had been giving the task her undivided attention.

Such behavior is common in contemporary Western society. Attention is a gift and a quality that many people just don't possess today. People are afraid of silence.

Would you agree with that observation? Many people always seem to want some noise going on. They want background music – something to distract them. Here is my point: if you want to hear God's voice, you can't afford to be distracted. You have to focus all of your heart and mind on God. You have to cultivate attention.

☙ "BOWING DOWN" OUR EAR

Second, we understand from the Scriptures that we must "bow down" or incline our ear. This means we must be humble and teachable. Many people read the Bible or pray to God with their own preconceptions. They believe they know what God should have said. They believe they know what God is going to say. If God has said or does say something different than what they have presupposed, they are simply unable to hear it. They are made deaf by their own presumptions.

Most people who belong to any kind of religious denomination read the Bible with their own denominational slant. They think, "Well, if it's not in my denomination's teaching, it isn't in the Bible." I don't believe there is any denomination for which that viewpoint is completely true. There are various truths in the Bible that we don't hear much about in our churches today. If we limit our hearing from God to only what we have heard in church, we will subject ourselves to a form of spiritual deafness. We will miss much of what God is saying to us.

❦ TIME AND QUIETNESS

After attention and humility, I would characterize the next two requirements as time and quietness, which are also often connected. How removed these two concepts seem to be from our contemporary culture! Most people today don't take time to be quiet. Yet this practice is referred to many times in the book of Psalms. For instance, Psalm 46:10 says,

> *Be still, and know that I am God.*

Out of stillness, we hear God's voice. An alternative translation of this verse reads,

> *Cease striving and know that I am God.* (NASB)

In the margin of the New American Standard Bible, there is a note that offers an additional rendering for the first part of this verse: "Let go, relax." If we combine the meanings presented by these two translations, we have the following: "Be still and know…"; "cease striving and know…"; "let go, relax, and know that I am God." To me, Psalm 46:10 speaks of quietness and relaxation – and that requires time. Most often, we hear from God when we take the time to wait for Him to speak to us.

Waiting is necessary because, as we have seen, God doesn't always speak the instant we begin the process of listening to Him. Psalm 62:1 seems to confirm this idea:

My soul waits in silence for God only.   (NASB)

David's words are profound: "My soul waits in silence for God only." We have to wait. We have to be silent. Our attention has to be focused on one Person alone – God.

Four verses later, David directly addresses his soul using the same words:

My soul, wait in silence for God only.
(Psalm 62:5 NASB)

Have you ever instructed your soul regarding how to wait? Have you ever said, "My soul, wait in silence for God only"? The emphasis is on waiting for God in silence. This means being in an attitude of attention, reverence, quietness, and relaxation – with our hearts and minds focused on the Lord. We will talk more about waiting in another section.

✎ WORSHIP

Let's now look at the fifth requirement for hearing God's voice. In my opinion, there is no better preparation through which we can achieve the kind of attitude that will enable us to hear the Lord than worship. This truth is beautifully brought out in Psalm 95, a portion of which we looked at in chapter 11:

Come, let us worship and bow down [again, the emphasis is on humility], let us kneel before the

*Lord our Maker. For He is our God, and we are
the people of His pasture and the sheep of His hand.
Today, if you would hear His voice, do not harden
your hearts....* (Psalm 95:6–8 NASB)

In this passage, we see again the warning against hardening our hearts if we want to hear God's voice. An excellent way to prepare our hearts is to follow what is outlined in Psalm 95:6–8:

- Let us worship God.
- Let us bow down before Him.
- Let us kneel before Him.
- Let us come to Him with reverence.
- Let us acknowledge His greatness, His majesty, His sovereignty, and His wisdom.
- Let us open our hearts to Him.

The Scriptures say, "The Lord is a great God" (Psalm 95:3 NASB). It is necessary for us to give the Lord all the respect and reverence of which we are capable. We need to appreciate the tremendous privilege of hearing from Him. Imagine! The Almighty God, the Creator and Sustainer of the universe, is willing to speak to you and me, individually. What a privilege!

In today's culture, there is little respect for authority. Even so, God still demands our respect. We must come to Him with reverence. We must approach Him with the kind of respect that is expressed in worship – humbling ourselves before Him; kneeling before Him, if need be; acknowledging His greatness; and opening our hearts to Him. With our worship, we begin to open ourselves to hear from God.

❧ WAITING

We have covered five important requirements for hearing from God: attention, humility, time, quietness, and worship. I want to present one more prerequisite: waiting. This requirement is closely linked with worship.

One of the most humbling responses required of us is to wait. Paul writes how the Thessalonians "turned to God from idols to serve a living and true God, and to wait for His Son from heaven" (1 Thessalonians 1:9–10). I find that statement very interesting. What does the Christian life consist of? First, serving the living God. Most of us would accept that mandate. But did you notice what is mentioned in the second part of the verse? Waiting for His Son. Jesus is coming back for a church that is waiting. In the providence of God, there will be a time when we will no longer be serving, but we will simply be waiting. We will have finished our service. But, after having served, we will need to wait.

What does waiting indicate? I want to suggest two significant features of waiting. First, it is a mark of faith. We are waiting because we believe God is going to intervene in our lives and in the world.

Picture a group of people by the side of the road.

Some are idly walking back and forth. Others are wandering aimlessly. Still others are just standing around listlessly. None of these people has any particular goal in mind. But one man is different from the rest of the group. He knows that the place by the side of the road where he is standing is a bus stop, and he has arrived at that place, at that time, because he desires to go in a specific direction. He is waiting in faith for the bus to arrive to take him there. His brand of purposeful waiting makes him unique compared with all the other people by the side of the road.

A second feature of waiting is that it signifies our dependence on God. I believe this is one of the most important lessons we must learn in life. We need to gladly acknowledge that we are totally dependent on the Lord. If God doesn't show up, our whole venture will be a failure.

Thus, waiting is an integral part of Christian discipline, demonstrating our faith in God and our utter dependence upon Him. It is an expression of our belief that the Lord will do what He says He will do, in His time. We cannot dictate the time frame in which God will do it. Thus, waiting is an acknowledgment of our reliance on Him. It is our declaration, "Lord, I can't do it. If You don't do it, it won't happen. I have to wait on You."

How long will we have to wait before God responds to our seeking Him? We really don't know. Have you ever noticed that when God submits you to a test, He very seldom tells you in advance how long it will last? We don't know whether we will have to hold out for six months or six years.

Unfortunately, at the end of a certain period of time, you may say, "Well, this is not working. I may as well give up." However, remember that if you give up, you might miss the answer you have been waiting for. The answer might actually be right around the corner. Can you see what the essence of this issue is for us? Dependence on God.

Are you facing a situation right now where you are waiting and relying upon the Lord for an answer? Are you ready to give up? I urge you to keep waiting. Let's conclude this chapter with a declaration that contains the six requirements for hearing from God – just to let Him know we continue to trust in Him:

Lord, I give You my full attention. I humble myself in Your presence. Take all the time You need. I will stay quiet before You. I will worship You, for You are worthy! I will wait in faith and dependence for You to speak the answer that I need to hear. Amen.

PART IV
Prepare the Way of the Lord

THIRTEEN

Meeting with God

As preparation for this chapter, I want to review some foundational points about hearing from God. First, we hear God's voice with our hearts, not with our physical ears. That is why we must cultivate sensitivity of heart. If we don't develop this sensitivity, we can become spiritually deaf. In the Scriptures, two words that describe the hearts of those who were spiritually deaf are calloused and hardened.

Next, there are six specific requirements for achieving the kind of sensitivity of heart we need in order to hear from God.

1. Attention
2. Humility
3. Time
4. Quietness
5. Worship
6. Waiting

We noted that David said, "My soul waits in silence for God only" (Psalm 62:1 NASB), and that the best preparation to begin this process is worship, as expressed beautifully in Psalm 95:6: "Come, let us worship and bow down, let us kneel before the Lord our Maker" (NASB). Psalm 95 also instructs us to be open before the Lord: "Today, if you would hear His voice, do not harden your hearts" (verses 7–8 NASB). The truth that I am going to address in this chapter follows naturally from the points we have just reviewed. Here is that truth: God sets the time and the place to answer us.

We need to give absolute priority to God above all of our own interests and activities. We may have our own plan. We may have aspirations we are excited about and goals we are eager to accomplish. But if we want to hear God's voice, we must be prepared to let go of our own agendas. We need to "let go and relax," as the psalmist said. God sets the time and place, and it may be different from the time or place we would choose.

Let us now consider the examples of three men who met with God and heard His voice according to the Lord's time and place: Moses, Elijah, and Jeremiah.

MOSES

We begin with an account from the life of Moses found in Numbers 7:89. This verse describes Moses going into the tabernacle that had been erected in the wilderness. Moses spoke with God, and God responded.

*When Moses entered the Tent of Meeting [the tab-
ernacle] to speak with the Lord, he heard the voice
speaking to him from between the two cherubim
above the atonement cover on the ark of the Testimony. And He spoke with him.*

(Numbers 7:89 NIV84)

Whenever I read this verse, a stillness always comes over my soul. In my mind, I can see that tabernacle out in the blazing sunshine of the desert. It is surrounded by dust and barrenness. Yet, inside, there is coolness, shade, and quietness. That picture always challenges me to get away from the heat, the dust, the busyness, and the activity of life. I want to come into a quiet place where I can speak with God and hear Him speak to me.

Do you see from this passage that there was a specific place where God spoke with Moses? It was behind the second veil of the tabernacle, from between the two cherubim in the Holy of Holies – the Most Holy Place. The holy nature of the location where God chose to speak with Moses shows us how sacred it is to hear the voice of the Lord ourselves.

The cherubim mentioned here are symbols of worship and fellowship. God spoke to Moses from a position just above the atonement cover on the ark of the testimony. This was the place where the blood of sacrifices, which spoke of covered and forgiven sin, had literally been sprinkled.

How significant all these points are! The Holy of Holies was a place of worship. It was a place of fellowship. It was a place where there was the eternal evidence of sin forgiven and covered. (This is very important because, in the next chapter, we will see that hidden and unforgiven sin will always keep us from hearing the voice of the Lord.) It was in this place of worship, fellowship, and forgiveness that Moses heard the voice of the Lord.

I am reminded of what Jesus said to His disciples in Matthew 6:6: "But you, when you pray, go into your inner room..." (NASB). Why go into an inner room? Surely, the intent would be to get away from all distractions and to shut out the sights and sounds of the world in order to be still before God. I believe every Christian should have some kind of inner room. A friend of mine used to go into a broom closet under the stairs in his house. Even though the closet was full of all types of cleaning supplies, that is the place where he heard from God. It became a sacred place for him.

ELIJAH

The second example of a man who heard God's voice in a particular time and place is the prophet Elijah. Elijah experienced tremendous personal triumph when he called down fire on the sacrifice at Mount Carmel, demonstrating to the false prophets of Baal and the Israelites who worshipped this idol that God alone is the true God. The prophets of Baal, who had been humbled and humiliated, were then executed at Elijah's command. But where do we find the prophet after this great victory? Running for his life from Jezebel, the queen.

Out in the wilderness to which he had fled, Elijah asked the Lord to take his life. Instead, God sent an angel to feed and strengthen him so that he was able to make it all the way to Mount Horeb. (See 1 Kings 18:17–39; 19:1–9.) This was the very place where God first made His covenant with Israel. Let's see what happened to Elijah when he arrived there:

> *The Lord said, "Go out and stand on the mountain in the presence of the Lord, for the Lord is about to pass by." Then a great and powerful wind tore the mountains apart and shattered the rocks before the Lord, but the Lord was not in the wind. After the wind there was an earthquake, but the Lord was not in the earthquake. After the earthquake came a fire, but the Lord was not in the fire.*
>
> (1 Kings 19:11–12 NIV84)

In this encounter, we see three tremendous demonstrations of God's power: wind that shattered the mountains, an earthquake, and a fire. It is significant that the Lord's voice wasn't in any of those manifestations of His might. Here are the next words in this passage:

> *And after the fire came a gentle whisper.*
>
> (1 Kings 19:12 NIV)

I previously stated that God doesn't shout. Even so, some people picture God as a big, loud man shouting. From the behavior I see among various world leaders, I think that many of them may picture God as a big man shouting. In reality, He is very different from that caricature. After all the demonstrations of His power, God revealed Himself through a gentle whisper – and that whisper impacted Elijah tremendously.

> *When Elijah heard it [not the wind, not the earthquake, and not the fire, but the gentle whisper], he pulled his cloak over his face and went out and stood at the mouth of the cave.*
>
> (1 Kings 19:13 NIV)

What did pulling his cloak over his face signify? It meant worship. It meant bowing. It indicated humbling himself and opening up his spirit to God. When Elijah was ready to listen, God responded:

> *Then a voice said to him, "What are you doing here, Elijah?"*
> (1 Kings 19:13 NIV)

Think of the careful preparation God had made for Elijah to hear His voice. Why? Because He is concerned that we hear what He wants to say to us. Please remember that the Lord may not be in the wind, the earthquake, or the fire. Yet, if you have ears to hear, there will be "a gentle whisper." When you hear that "gentle whisper," that "still small voice" (KJV, NKJV), you will want to pull your cloak over your face. You will want to worship. Your heart will want to bow down.

It is important to see what happened to Elijah when he heard God's gentle whisper. When he went to Horeb, he was really a beaten man. He was ready to give up, to quit, to throw in the towel. But after he heard God's voice, he was a restored prophet who had received strength and a new focus and direction for his ministry.

Up to that time, Elijah didn't know what to do next. But hearing God's voice gave him fresh instructions for his ministry. The same results can happen for you and me. Strength and new direction can come to us from hearing God's voice.

JEREMIAH

A third man who heard the voice of God is Jeremiah, whom the Lord instructed to go to a particular location:

> *This is the word that came to Jeremiah from the Lord: "Go down to the potter's house, and there I will give you My message."* (Jeremiah 18:1 NIV)

God said to Jeremiah, in effect, "If you want to hear My voice, you have to be in a certain place. I'm going to speak to you. But you must be in the right place at the right time." We see from this passage that Jeremiah obeyed God's directions:

*I went down to the potter's house, and I saw him
[the potter] working at the wheel. But the pot he
was shaping from the clay was marred in his hands;
so the potter formed it into another pot, shaping it
as seemed best to him. Then the word of the Lord
came to me. He said, "Can I not do with you, Israel,
as this potter does?" declares the Lord. "Like clay in
the hand of the potter, so are you in my hand, Israel."*

(Jeremiah 18:3–6 NIV)

Do you see why there was a time and a place? The
potter's house was where God wanted Jeremiah to be
so he could see what the potter was doing with the pot
on the wheel. The potter working on the clay pot was
a symbol of how God was going to deal with Israel –
and how God is dealing with Israel, for the message
of Jeremiah 18 continues to be applicable today. Please
remember that Israel is still that pot in God's hands. The
Lord is shaping Abraham's descendants on the wheels
of circumstance and history right now.

God made an appointment with Jeremiah and
said, "If you'll go to the potter's house, I'll speak to
you." Clearly, Jeremiah couldn't receive the message
God wanted to give him until he was in the right place.
He had to obey. He had to be at the designated site.

One other point to notice from this passage is that
before Jeremiah could have a message for others, he
himself had to hear from God. It has always perplexed

me that while Bible schools and seminaries seem to spend so much time training people how to speak, seldom do these institutions train people how to hear. This is the truth of the matter: if you have never heard from God, you really have nothing to say. Believe me, an individual who has heard from God is worth listening to – even if they don't have all the fine points of homiletics. Today, people want to listen to someone who has heard from God.

A CLIFFTOP IN DENMARK

Some years ago, I was in Denmark, which is the native country of my first wife, Lydia. The Lord very clearly directed me to go to a certain clifftop overlooking what the Danes call the Western Sea, and what the British call the North Sea. It was a fine winter afternoon, and I was there just as the sun was going down in the western sky.

As I climbed, the rays of the setting sun were falling across the water and shining into my face. When I got to the top of the cliff, I quieted my heart before God while I looked out at the sea. In that time, the Lord spoke to me for about an hour. He showed me that the conduct of the sea, the way the sea's waves behaved, was like the history of the church. The church had started at high tide, but gradually the waters went out and there was low tide – the Dark Ages. Then, the tide turned, and the waters began to come in again. But they came in wave by wave, one great move of the Spirit after another.

God showed me what is going to happen as the church age comes to its climax. I have never felt free to publicly share much of what He revealed to me. However, I was able to receive all of what God wanted to show me because I kept an appointment with Him on a clifftop overlooking the North Sea. God set the time and place, and I obeyed.

That was a life-changing encounter for me, and here is my advice to you as a result: please be expectant and listen for any appointments the Lord wants to set up with you.

FOURTEEN

Confession Removes Barriers to Hearing

Most Christians would readily admit there are various barriers that can keep us from hearing the voice of God. In the next chapters, we will focus on removing some of these barriers. I believe one of the greatest barriers between God and human beings is pride. I don't think we sufficiently understand the nature of this hindrance. The first sin in the history of the universe was not drunkenness, immorality, or even murder. It was pride. What's more, that sin did not take place on earth; it took place in heaven when Lucifer (Satan) rebelled against God, desiring to exalt himself above the Lord. All other sins have followed this original act of pride.

If we can deal effectively with pride, there probably will not be any other sin we can't deal with. But if we do not deal with pride, it will keep us from dealing with many other sins.

I want to suggest some very simple ways to remove this barrier. The most important principles in the spiritual life are nearly always simple. But sometimes simple can seem to be very difficult! Sometimes, it takes a lot of help from God to bring us to the place of simplicity.

CONFESSION TO GOD

The first step we can take to humble ourselves before God is to confess our sins. First John 1:9 says,

If we confess our sins, He [God] is faithful and just to forgive us our sins and to cleanse us from all unrighteousness.

GOD WANTS TO FORGIVE YOU

Let me emphasize that God does not want to hold your sins against you. Through Christ, He has made total provision for you to be completely forgiven and cleansed. But the Lord has laid down a condition: "If we confess our sins...." (1 John 1:9).

If we do not confess our sins, those transgressions continue to be reckoned or counted against us. The only way we can escape from the consequences and guilt of our sins is by confessing them. We simply must acknowledge, "Yes, God, I did this. It's true."

In this matter of confession, I would urge you not to start a process of self-examination. The more you examine your life, the less pleased you will be with yourself. That is not the right way for us to approach our sins. Instead, for this purpose, God has given us an Examiner. Do you know who He is? The Holy Spirit.

In John 16:8, Jesus said, "And when He [the Holy Spirit] has come, He will convict the world of sin, and of righteousness, and of judgment." This verse speaks of three eternal realities on which all true religion is based: sin, righteousness, and judgment.

First John further says, "All unrighteousness is sin" (1 John 5:17). If you know what straight is, then you also know what crooked is. Anything that is not straight is crooked. There may be varying degrees of crookedness, but when something is crooked, you can't escape that fact. It is the same with righteousness and sin. Anything that is not righteous is sinful. There are only two categories, without a lot of different shades of gray. It is either righteousness or sin – and the Holy Spirit is the One who convicts us of sin.

✤ RELIEF FROM GUILT

Satan strives to make you feel guilty. He always leaves you wondering, "Have I done enough to be forgiven? Should I have done more? Was that all that was required?" But the Holy Spirit doesn't do that. He says, "This is what you did wrong; this is what you have to do to be cleared of it." He is very specific; He doesn't leave any blurred edges. The Spirit doesn't leave any room for

Satan to come in with unfair accusations. Please let the truth of 1 John 1:9 soak into your spirit: "If we confess our sins, He is faithful and just to forgive us our sins."

With all the power I have, I want to emphasize this point again: God wants to forgive your sins. He does not want to hold your sins against you. He does not want you to go around feeling guilty. By His design, there is one step to take: You have to confess. You have to say, "Yes, I did it. I did it."

If you open yourself to the Holy Spirit and give God time to reveal your wrongdoings, believe me, He will reveal them to you. He will bring up events you may have forgotten and behaviors you never even thought were sinful – but He will show them to you from His perspective.

This process has sometimes been difficult for me, but not because I had committed enormous sins. It was the fact that my sins seemed so stupid and petty. I have found myself saying, "How could I ever have said or done something like that?"

I believe that if we confess our sins and receive God's forgiveness, we will never have to account for those sins again – ever. However, if we do not confess them, one day, we are going to have to answer to God for them. I have always found it embarrassing to privately tell God what I have done. But think of how much more embarrassing it will be if, one day, the whole universe hears what we have done.

❧ CONFESSION TO ONE ANOTHER

A second remedy for removing the barrier of pride through confession is similar to the first. It is also just as simple. We find this remedy in James 5:16: "Confess your sins to each other and pray for each other so that you may be healed" (NIV). To me, it is very clear from this context that unconfessed sin is a barrier to healing. In fact, it is probably the most common single barrier to healing.

I don't know whether you have ever noticed, but people who have just received salvation are also easily able to receive healing. They come forward as repentant sinners, believing they don't deserve anything – yet, they are forgiven and they are healed. Do you know why this happens so frequently? Because these repentant sinners have no barriers left. At that moment, every sin they have ever committed has been forgiven, and they are fully open to whatever they can receive from the Lord.

Unfortunately, as we go on in the Christian life, unless we are very watchful and careful, we can accumulate sins that we have not confessed. Then, when we go to God for healing, a barrier of unforgiven sin keeps us from receiving what we seek. This is why James says, "Confess your sins to each other."

It is humbling to confess your sins to God. But, believe me, it is even more humbling to confess your sins to another person. Even so, when conducted in the context of a trusting relationship, it is a very healthy form of self-humbling.

❦ CONFESSION AMONG LEADERS

Some years ago, I was in Hull, a small city in England, to conduct a series of meetings. At the end of these meetings, I called the leaders up on the platform and prayed for them. Through that session, God ministered to them, so the group urged me to come back, and I did. As a result of those initial meetings, these leaders, representing perhaps fifteen churches, have been meeting together for four years and waiting on God. To me, that is an almost unbelievable phenomenon.

In a way, my second series of meetings with this group was different from almost any other meetings where I have ministered. Not because I was different, but because the atmosphere was different. Something had changed in the environment as a result of the openness of these leaders.

I preached some very direct messages, emphasizing that only the sins we confess are forgiven. God is fully ready and waiting to forgive us, but He has laid down this one condition: if we confess our sins, He is faithful and just to forgive them.

At the conclusion of the meetings, I issued a challenge. Without any emotion or hype, I said to the audience, "Now, if you need to confess sins, you can confess them to God. But the Bible also says to confess your sins to one another so that you may be healed. One major barrier to healing is unconfessed sin. With that understanding, I invite you to come down to the front to pray together. You're free to come down."

In response to that invitation, about ten couples walked to the front and spent about two hours confessing their sins to one another. The group included some well-known leaders from that area. I felt this was very significant. I regard their response as the lasting fruit produced by their waiting on God. Barriers were broken down as a result.

ꙮ CONFESSION BETWEEN HUSBANDS AND WIVES

I believe it is especially healthy for husbands and wives to confess their sins to each other. Some years ago, I was ministering to a Christian man who really wanted to serve the Lord.

But he was struggling with a tendency to become unreasonably angry toward his wife and children.

"Well," I said, "one thing I would recommend is the following practice: every time you lose your temper in the presence of your wife and children, you ought to specifically confess that as a sin to them. I believe the mere thought that you are going to have to repent to them will inhibit you from losing your temper the next time." I think that suggestion made a big difference to that family.

In confession between husbands and wives, one of

the keys to success is to open yourselves up to God and give Him time to reveal what you should be repenting of. As I said previously, it is beneficial to first try to relax for a little while and start listening. Let God speak to you, and when He does, follow through with what He shows you to confess to each other.

I think many marriages would be healed if a husband and wife would humble themselves before each other and confess their sins. A husband could say to his wife, "I'm sorry I lost my temper. I shouldn't have spoken to you like that. I had no right to be so critical and unkind. Please forgive me."

Do you know what such a confession deals with? Pride and male chauvinism. Many men would never humble themselves before their wives. I believe this refusal has a lot to do with the male ego. It is rather common for men to behave in a chauvinistic manner when relating to women and dealing with other situations. But this behavior is not from God.

GOD'S LOVING PRESENCE

You may be saying to yourself, "I don't think I have any unconfessed sins." That is wonderful! But my question to you is, "How close are you to God?" If you were to spend a little time waiting in the presence of the Lord, your perspective might change dramatically.

I am sharing these principles on confession of sin out of personal experience, so in no way am I pointing a finger. I have never been a "backslider," falling away from God into a lifestyle of sin. I have faithfully served the Lord for more than fifty years. By the grace of God, my wife and I have seen uncounted numbers of people helped through our ministry. But remember that, during our sabbatical, when Ruth and I got alone with God without any premeditated plan or agenda, it took the Lord nearly six months to clear up the debris in my life.

God showed me incidents that occurred over the past thirty years. He would put His finger on a situation I had forgotten about, and He would say, "You never confessed it." As a mutual act of humility, Ruth and I would confess our sins to one another. It might not always be necessary to confess in that way, but the Bible does say to confess your sins one to one another. Ruth and I practice this command, and it helps to keep us humble.

How would you feel about confessing your sins to another person within a trusting relationship? One factor that might be preventing you from obeying this requirement is pride. As I previously pointed out, pride is one of the greatest barriers to hearing from God. We will talk about this topic further in a later chapter, "Choosing Humility."

FIFTEEN

Results of Corporate Confession

We have seen the importance of confessing our sins to one another in the context of a trusting relationship. Let us now look at two additional results of corporate confession.

REVIVAL AND CHURCH-PLANTING

In my ministry throughout the body of Christ, I hear a lot of prophecies about a coming revival. I may even have given some of those prophecies myself. But one fact is irrefutable: we don't have revival until we have it. Furthermore, we will not experience revival until we have met the conditions.

We can have prophecy after prophecy predicting an awakening, but a real barrier to revival is unconfessed sin. Until that barrier is dealt with, no amount of preaching, singing, or publicity will bring revival. Unless we have addressed this issue, our progress toward revival will remain disappointing.

Many years ago, I read the journals of John Wesley. In one of his entries, I discovered a comment he made about one of the strongest Methodist societies known to him. He said that it had grown out of ten people who committed themselves to meet weekly to confess their faults to one another.

That is not the modern plan for starting a church, is it? Yet the Methodist movement ended up impacting all of Britain and most of the United States for a century. So, maybe there is something to be said for starting a movement that way.

WALKING IN THE LIGHT

Another beneficial result of confessing our sins is found in Isaiah 59:1–2:

> *Behold, the Lord's hand is not shortened, that it*
> *cannot save; nor His ear heavy, that it cannot hear.*
> *But your iniquities have separated you from your*
> *God; and your sins have hidden His face from you,*
> *so that He will not hear.*

It is encouraging to know that God still has excellent hearing and His arm is still powerful! It is also encouraging to know that the Lord does not show partiality. Each and every one of us has the right to access God through the cleansing blood of Jesus. But we often overlook this crucial truth: the blood doesn't cleanse those who don't confess.

The importance of meeting God's conditions for forgiveness can be seen clearly in the following passage:

> *If we say that we have fellowship with Him, and walk in darkness, we lie and do not practice the truth. But if we walk in the light as He is in the light, we have fellowship with one another, and the blood of Jesus Christ His Son cleanses us from all sin.*
>
> (1 John 1:6–7)

In verse 7, there are three verbs in the continuing present tense. If we continually walk in the light, we continually have fellowship with one another, and the blood continually cleanses us.

Note that these results are conditional. The first word is if: "If we walk in the light...."

Here is my comment on the necessity of meeting that condition: if we are out of fellowship, we are out of the light. If we are out of fellowship, the blood is not cleansing us. The blood does not cleanse in the dark; it only cleanses in the light. Thus, if we are in the dark but want to be cleansed, we must come to the light. "If we walk in the light as He is in the light, we have fellowship with one another, and the blood of Jesus Christ His Son cleanses us from all sin."

The lesson is clear: as we remove the barriers of sin and pride from our lives, we open the way to hear from the Lord. This happens both when we seek the Lord individually and when we seek Him corporately.

It is very important to remember, however, that our primary reason for coming to the Lord should not be to receive all His blessings and benefits. Our primary motivation for coming must be because of who He is. First and foremost, hearing from God is about relationship. Any blessing or benefit that follows is as a result of our relationship and connection to the Head, our Lord Jesus Christ.

SIXTEEN
Choosing Humility

To effectively deal with pride, I have suggested not only confessing our sins to God, but also confessing our sins to one another. We looked at the examples of confession among leaders, confession between husbands and wives, corporate confession, and confession in other trustworthy relationships. Such confession requires humility.

Another way to humble ourselves is to submit to God when He deals with a particular issue in our lives, trusting in His faithfulness and righteousness. Moses proclaimed,

> *Ascribe greatness to our God! The Rock! His work is perfect, for all His ways are just; a God of faithfulness and without injustice, righteous and upright is He.* (Deuteronomy 32:3–4 NASB)

When we are under pressure, it is easy to begin to blame the Lord, saying, for example, "God, You haven't treated me right. You haven't answered my prayers. I should have been married by now. Why didn't You send me a spouse?" It is not God's fault. He has plans for us that are different from our own. If He has a spouse for you, He will work it out in His own timing.

It is very important to understand that God is totally just and trustworthy.

Please do not entertain the thought that God has ever been unjust or unfair. He never is. We need to set aside the idea that the Lord owes us something that He has yet to give. It will make all the difference in our approach to Him. "His work is perfect." He never makes a mistake. "All His ways are just." He is "a God of faithfulness and without injustice." Can you say "Amen" to that?

HUMBLE YOURSELF

It may encourage you to know that, as we progress in the Christian life, all of us will experience periods when everything seems to be going wrong. We will endure situations that don't work out the way we feel they should. Our finances might become tight, our expectations might not be met, or our friends might let us down. What do we do during these times? How should we respond? The apostle Peter says it best:

Therefore humble yourselves under the mighty hand of God, that He may exalt you in due time.

(1 Peter 5:6)

When life is not going the way you expect, you must humble yourself. You need to release the situation to the Lord, saying, "God, I don't understand what's going on, but I know You are perfectly just. You never make a mistake. What You are doing is right. I submit to Your dealings. Teach me what I don't know. Help me to learn what I need to understand. I am willing to learn."

UNEXPECTED CHALLENGES

When God brought the Israelites out of Egypt, He dealt with them by allowing them to experience an outbreak of unexpected challenges. He permitted them to go through circumstances that were designed to humble them. Looking at just two verses from Deuteronomy 8 will help us to better understand God's purposes in this process. Moses is speaking to the Israelites after they had finished their journey through the wilderness:

> You shall remember that the Lord your God led you all the way these forty years in the wilderness, to humble you and test you, to know what was in your heart, whether you would keep His commandments or not. So He humbled you, allowed you to hunger, and fed you with manna which you did not know nor did your fathers know.
>
> (Deuteronomy 8:2–3)

How did the Lord humble the Israelites? By allowing them to go through times of need and insufficiency – times when their main desires were not being satisfied.

Why did God do this? What was His purpose? To humble them.

Did He succeed? No, not really. The generation that perished in the wilderness didn't learn to humble themselves. They complained, they murmured, they rebelled, they blamed God – and, as a result, they were refused entry into the promised land.

Please allow me to give you this helpful piece of advice: when you are going through a hard time, don't complain and don't murmur. Don't say, "God, I can't take this. You're not treating me right." Why should you avoid such complaining? Because it can cause you to miss the purpose of God. God's purpose in the trials you face is to humble you. If you will humble yourself, then God's purpose will be fulfilled.

HUMILITY IS A CHOICE

I remember the first time God specifically spoke to my first wife, Lydia, and me about this matter of humbling ourselves in difficult circumstances. In 1948, we had to leave Israel with our eight girls on one of the last convoys out of the region during the Israeli War of Independence. We arrived in Britain, my native country, as refugees. Our family did not yet have a home, so we had to split up our family, sending our girls to live with other families for a period of time. We were miserable! Yet, in the midst of this trying time, the Lord prophetically spoke to us and said, "Humble yourselves under the mighty hand of God." I have to admit, it took a long while for me to be able to do this, but it was a necessary step. When everything is going wrong, when it seems as if your prayers are not being answered, then humble yourself before the Lord, asking Him to show you where you need to change and what you need to know and do.

JOB'S EXAMPLE

The following is another passage of Scripture that has been impressed upon me regarding our proper response to God during difficulties. In this passage, Job asks the Lord an amazing question:

> *What is man that You magnify him, and that You are concerned about him?* (Job 7:17 NASB)

Do you realize that God has a magnifying glass – and He scrutinizes us through this glass? He doesn't just look at us the way we are. He brings everything into magnification. Job continues,

> *What is man…that You should visit him every morning, and test him every moment?*
> (Job 7:17–18)

Were you aware that God visits you every morning? And were you aware that God tests you every moment? Are you prepared for His daily visitations and tests?

God is continually testing us to see whether we will

be faithful and obedient or rebellious and disobedient. You and I have no choice about this process. God doesn't say, "Well, if you'll permit Me, I'll test you." No, God just tests us.

I know God visits me every morning, and I try to be ready for His visitation. I try to keep myself in a frame of mind where I will pass His tests. Whatever He has to say, whatever He wants to change in me – whatever correction or new direction He wants to give me – I want to be ready to receive it.

STRAIGHT AND TRUE

In the Lord's dealings with me, He has clearly demonstrated this characteristic: He means exactly what He says. He doesn't exaggerate. Everything He states is absolutely correct. Some Christians haven't studied the fine print in the contract they have made with God. They may be looking for an exemption to His words, not realizing God doesn't work that way.

Suppose, for example, you were in a car accident. You go to see the claims agent at your insurance company, and they ask, "Well, who was driving?"

"Our daughter was driving."

"How old is she?"

"Well, she was twenty-four at the time."

They say, "Our conditions specifically state that no driver of this car can be under the age of twenty-five."

"So, what does that mean for this accident?"
"We're not going to pay your claim."
"You mean, just because of the difference of one year, you won't pay?"
"That's right. That's exactly the way it is."

In many ways, that is how it is with God. He means exactly what He says. When He lays down conditions, they are not approximations. They are not generalities. He is absolutely specific as to what He requires. When they face a difficulty, many people tend to say, "Well, God didn't deliver." But His response is, "You didn't meet the conditions. You didn't read the fine print."

Is God is dealing with you right now? Do you feel as if He has visited you this morning and is testing You every moment? I encourage you to respond to Him with the following prayer of humility:

Lord, in all of these tests I'm facing, I humble myself before You. Show me where I am wrong and what condition I need to meet. Help me to learn what I need to know and do. I want to be obedient and submissive. In this moment, I choose humility. In Jesus's name, amen.

SEVENTEEN

Preparing for God's Glory

Previously, we talked about prophecies of a coming revival and how a significant barrier to awakening is unconfessed sin. I believe God is asking us to prepare the way for Him to visit us. I have confidence that God will visit the church in our nations. I am not saying He will visit the nations – but I believe He will visit the church in each nation. We don't know when He will do this. The timing for His visitation is totally a matter of His sovereignty. However, the Scriptures make it very clear that we have to get ready for His coming. We have to prepare the way of the Lord.

PREPARING THE WAY

The following verses from Isaiah 40 give us instructions for that preparation. The words recorded in this passage were later applied to John the Baptist as he prepared the way for the ministry of Jesus. (See Matthew 3:1–3.)

> *The voice of one crying in the wilderness: "Pre-pare the way of the Lord; make straight in the desert a highway for our God. Every valley shall be exalted and every mountain and hill brought low; the crooked places shall be made straight and the rough places smooth; the glory of the Lord shall be revealed, and all flesh shall see it together; for the mouth of the Lord has spoken."* (Isaiah 40:3–5)

What is the result of this promise? "The glory of the Lord shall be revealed, and all flesh shall see it together." But what are the steps of preparation? How do we prepare the way of the Lord? Again, we must remove the hindrances that keep God from accomplishing what He wants to in our lives. The indication from Isaiah 40 is that as we remove these hindrances, we will experience four changes:

1. "Every valley shall be exalted," or lifted up. I believe this may refer to the "low" qualities that many people despise today, like modesty, chastity, self-effacement, a willingness to serve, and a willingness to be in the background. It is those "valley concepts" that have to be lifted up in our day.

2. "Every mountain and hill [shall be] brought low." Just as the "low concepts" must be raised up, the "high beliefs" have to be brought down. All of our

hype, exaggeration, and boasting has to be brought low. Our tendency toward self-glorification, self-exaltation, self-promotion – even, in religious circles, our tendency toward wanting to appear super-spiritual – has to come down. God will not push His way through those mountains. They must be brought low to make a way for Him.

3. "The crooked places shall be made straight." Let me just bluntly ask you: are there crooked areas in your life? How do you deal with money? What about when you fill out your income tax return? It is not difficult to cheat on a tax return – but to do so is crooked. God says, "If you want Me to visit you, you will have to straighten out that crookedness."

4. "The rough places [shall be made] smooth." Do you have rough places in your life? Do you react angrily when things don't go the way you want, or when you're challenged, or when somebody disagrees with you? Do you engage in self-justification or argumentativeness, where you say, "Well, it's not my fault. He did the wrong thing," or "Our church is perfect. It's the other churches that need to be straightened out"? In God's sight, to bring forth revival, all of those rough places have to be smoothed out.

THE GLORY REVEALED

The glory of the Lord will be revealed. Do you believe that? I certainly do, because I know that God keeps His

Word. He is faithful. But His glory will only be revealed through those who have met His conditions:

- The valleys have to be exalted.
- The mountains have to be brought low.
- The crooked places have to be made straight.
- The rough places have to be made smooth.

I believe the Lord is in the process of transforming us to fulfill the words of Isaiah 40. The above activities are on His agenda for the church in every nation in these pivotal days. Because God is in this process, we need to expect trials and tribulations. For some people, the tests and trials have already begun. For others, they are just ahead. We must recognize that if we don't pass the tests, we won't be ready to receive the revelation of God's glory.

In many ways, it is up to us: we need to determine whether we will be channels for the Lord's glory or whether we will allow the mountains to hold it back. If and when we meet God's conditions, His glory will be revealed. But where we refuse, He will withhold His glory.

PASSING THE TESTS

Let me simply say that testing doesn't end after the first few years of your Christian experience. Even after I had completed fifty years of Christian living, the tests continued. In some ways, these later tests have been harder than any others in my life. But by the grace of God – and I want to say this carefully – I believe I have passed the tests up to this time. That doesn't mean I have arrived. It simply means I am in line for the next test, presenting myself to be a useful tool in God's hands.

The promise of Job 7:18, which we looked at in the previous chapter, is true: God visits us every morning and tests us every moment. The Lord will never use anyone or anything that is untested. So, if you want to be used by God, you have to be tested. If you pass the test, He will use you for His glory.

This whole process is closely related to hearing God's voice of direction for us. Why? So we may move forward confidently and surely in His purposes for our lives. That will be the theme of our next chapter.

EIGHTEEN
How Can We Be Sure?

As I have stated throughout this book, in my own experience, hearing God's voice correctly has been the key factor in achieving true spiritual success. I now want to explore an extremely important, practical question that is directly related to this topic: How can we be sure we have really heard God's voice?

There are four kinds of confirmation that we should always look for to verify we have correctly heard from God. In this chapter, we will discuss the first three types of confirmation, and in chapter 19, we will look at the fourth form of corroboration.

AGREEMENT WITH SCRIPTURE

The first confirmation is agreement with Scripture. Does what we have heard align with the Spirit and the tenor of Scripture? Such affirmations are of supreme importance.

In this regard, let me present two interrelated facts. Number one: it is the Holy Spirit who brings God's voice to us. Number two: the Holy Spirit is the Author of all Scripture. This truth is stated in many passages of the Bible, but I will just quote one here:

> *All Scripture is inspired by God and profitable for teaching, for reproof, for correction, for training in righteousness.* (2 Timothy 3:16 NASB)

"Inspired by God" carries with it the implication that it was the Holy Spirit who motivated and directed the writers of Scripture. This helps us to understand that the Holy Spirit is the ultimate Author of all Scripture. Behind the human writers, there is one divine Person responsible for the accuracy and authority of Scripture. That divine Person is the Holy Spirit.

Now, let's put those two facts together. It is the Holy Spirit who brings God's voice to us, and it is the Holy Spirit who is the Author of all Scripture. We know that the Spirit never contradicts Himself, so He will never bring us a rhema word that does not agree with Scripture.

Having this understanding clearly in mind, the first way to be sure you have heard the voice of the Lord is to check what you believe you have received from God against the Scriptures. Does it agree with the words, with the Spirit, and with the principles of the Bible? If not, you can be sure it was not God's voice that you heard. It stands to reason that we can only test what we hear against Scripture if we know what the Scriptures say. So, knowing the Word of God must become a priority for us – we must read and study the Bible.

✎ REJECTING THE COUNTERFEITS

One reason we need to be very careful to test what we hear is that Satan has many counterfeits for the voice of the Lord. In the midst of today's culture and circumstances, it is necessary to know Satan's counterfeits and how to reject them. A passage in Isaiah states this fact very clearly:

> *When someone tells you to consult mediums and spiritists, who whisper and mutter, should not a people inquire of their God? Why consult the dead on behalf of the living? Consult God's instruction and the testimony of warning. If anyone does not speak according to this word, they have no light of dawn.* (Isaiah 8:19–20 NIV)

According to this passage, the consultants listed at the beginning of verse 19 are in the dark. God is warning us not to seek guidance from such advisors. Not only that, but He also lets us know what form of judgment is placed on those who bring messages, or listen to messages, that are not from Him:

> *Distressed and hungry, they will roam through the land; when they are famished, they will become*

*enraged and, looking upward, will curse their king
and their God. Then they will look toward the
earth and see only distress and darkness and fearful
gloom, and they will be thrust into utter darkness.*
(Isaiah 8:21–22 NIV)

What a terrible list of results we find at the end of
this verse: "distress," "darkness," "fearful gloom," "utter
darkness." These are the outcomes of listening to Satan's
counterfeits and being deceived. I believe the world is
filled with these counterfeits.

✎ AVOIDING DECEPTION

It would take a long time to list all the types of deception
that Satan uses, so I will mention only a few of them.
First on the list are mediums and spiritists (as mentioned in Isaiah 8), as well as fortune-tellers. Then there
are horoscopes, Ouija boards, tarot cards, teacup read-
ings, and various forms of so-called "mental science."

Believe me, when I warn against being deceived, I
am speaking from experience. Before I came to know
the Lord Jesus, I was deeply involved in yoga. I know
the darkness I was in during that time. Because of my
involvement in this philosophy, I went through quite a
struggle when I turned from that darkness to the light
of Jesus Christ and the truth of Scripture.

What is the end for those who follow such counterfeits? Let me quote again these words from Isaiah:

"They will...see only distress and darkness and fearful gloom, and they will be thrust into utter darkness" (Isaiah 8:22 NIV).

In contrast to those fearful ends, if we walk according to the Scriptures, we will have light. This truth is expressed in Psalm 119:105:

Your word is a lamp to my feet and a light to my path.

We never walk in the dark when we walk according to Scripture. We may not be able to see very far ahead, but we will always have enough light for our path and for the next step to take. This is what we need to remember as the first and most vital confirmation of what we believe to be God's voice: what we have heard must be in total agreement with Scripture.

CIRCUMSTANCES LINING UP

The second form of confirmation is when circumstances line up with the message. Sometimes, God asks us to do something strange or unexpected. We are wondering whether it really was the Lord, but then circumstances confirm it. The situation works out in such a way that we know God foresaw it and had it all prepared.

"THIS WAS THE WORD OF THE LORD"

For further insight on this topic, let's look at an example from the life of the prophet Jeremiah when he was in prison and the city of Jerusalem was being besieged.

Jeremiah had prophesied that the city would be taken and the land would be ravaged by the Babylonian army. He had predicted there would be destruction and distress everywhere. Yet, having actually prophesied these events himself, while he was in prison he heard a most amazing word from God:

> *The word of the Lord came to me: Hanamel son of Shallum your uncle is going to come to you and say, "Buy my field at Anathoth, because as nearest relative it is your right and duty to buy it."*
>
> (Jeremiah 32:6–7 NIV)

At that moment, the field was worth nothing. It would have had no real estate value in besieged Israel. There was no reason to buy a field that was inevitably going to be overrun and ravaged by the Babylonians. So, this was a surprising instruction from God. Jeremiah continues:

> *Then, just as the Lord had said, my cousin Hanamel came to me in the courtyard of the guard and said, "Buy my field at Anathoth in the territory of Benjamin. Since it is your right to redeem it and possess it, buy it for yourself."*   (Jeremiah 32:8 NIV)

Please take note of what Jeremiah says in response:

> *I knew that this was the word of the Lord; so I bought the field at Anathoth from my cousin Hanamel.*   (Jeremiah 32:9 NIV)

Let me repeat Jeremiah's statement of conviction: "I knew that this was the word of the Lord." God had spoken something astonishing and improbable to His prophet. Jeremiah wasn't quite sure about this word, but he kept it in his pending file, so to speak. Shortly after hearing the message, something happened that let Jeremiah know he had indeed heard the word of the Lord. Just as God had said, Jeremiah's relative did come to the prison, and he did ask Jeremiah to buy the very field the Lord had spoken about. That is what I call the confirmation of circumstance.

DIVINE PROMPTINGS

Let me give a couple of illustrations to show what you might encounter in your own life along these lines. Let's say you sense a prompting to buy a house in your area. The house isn't even up for sale, but you go and knock on the door to inquire about it. You introduce yourself to the woman who answers and politely say to her, "I live nearby, and if you should ever put your house up for sale, I would be interested in buying it from you."

The woman's response might be, "Isn't that amazing! My husband and I have just decided to sell our house, but we haven't yet had time to put it on the market." The prompting you had was the word of the Lord to you. The response you received from the woman was the confirmation of circumstances.

Or, suppose you are a business executive in a certain

city with a good home and an excellent position. One day, the Lord speaks to you about moving to a different city, and you can't comprehend why He would want you to make such a change. You pray, "Lord, I don't understand this, but if it is Your word for me and my family, please make it clear to me." The next day, your boss calls you into his office and offers you a transfer to the very city where you felt God wanted you to move – plus a raise in salary.

What are you going to make of this situation? Like Jeremiah, you will say, "I knew that this was the word of the Lord."

PEACE IN OUR HEART

What is the third important confirmation we should look for when we believe we have heard God's voice? We should expect and experience a peace in our heart. God's voice will always produce God's peace.

> *Let the peace of Christ rule in your hearts, to which indeed you were called in one body; and be thankful. Let the word of Christ richly dwell within you, with all wisdom teaching and admonishing one another with psalms and hymns and spiritual songs, singing with thankfulness in your hearts to God.*
>
> (Colossians 3:15–16 NASB)

❧ AN INWARD UMPIRE

The key phrase in this passage comes at the beginning of verse 15: "Let the peace of Christ rule in your hearts." The Greek word translated "rule" means to act as an arbiter or an umpire – making certain decisions and judgments, determining whether something is right or wrong. The Amplified Bible has a very good translation of this verse:

> Let the peace (soul harmony which comes) from Christ rule (act as umpire continually) in your hearts [deciding and settling with finality all questions that arise in your minds, in that peaceful state].
> (Colossians 3:15 AMPC)

Do you see the principle here? We have an inward umpire, an arbiter, who decides questions that we cannot decide. That umpire and arbiter is the peace of God. When the peace of God says yes, it is right. But when the peace of God is absent, we have to be cautious. We need to say, "Well, God, if this is from You, please let there be peace in my heart."

If there is unrest and struggling within you, and particularly if you feel pressured to act hastily, then be on your guard. Caution is needed when it is apparent that God's peace has been withdrawn. Usually, when peace is absent, God is trying to say to us, "You didn't hear Me right," or "You're not applying what I said correctly."

❦ THREE COMBINED FACTORS

The following three factors from the passage in Colossians 3 work together to confirm you have heard God's voice: the peace of Christ, thankfulness, and God's Word in your heart. The voice of God will be accompanied by peace, and you will be filled with thankfulness.

If it becomes a challenge or struggle to thank God in regard to what you have heard, that is a clear warning sign. If your praise dries up, then it is probably not the Holy Spirit who is moving in you. Remember that you are to "let the word of Christ richly dwell within you" (Colossians 3:16 NASB). Whatever the situation, make sure you are continually checking against Scripture what you think may be God's direction and purpose.

Let's conclude by reviewing the three ways we should look for confirmation if we really think we have heard the voice of God:

1. Agreement with Scripture. The Holy Spirit, who is the Author of Scripture, brings God's voice to us. He will never contradict Himself. The Spirit will never say something to us that disagrees with what He has already said in Scripture.

2. Circumstances lining up. In one way or another, the situation will work out so that we will know God is in it.

3. Peace in our heart. We will sense God's peace as an

umpire and arbiter, saying, "Yes, this is right. No, that is wrong."

In our final chapter, we will look at one further way of confirming we have heard God's voice: corroboration through our fellow believers.

NINETEEN

Clear Confirmations

We see God demonstrating His initiative and guidance in believers' lives when the church at Antioch sent out Barnabas and Saul (who later became known as Paul) for apostolic ministry:

> *In the church at Antioch there were prophets and teachers: Barnabas, Simeon called Niger, Lucius of Cyrene, Manaen (who had been brought up with Herod the tetrarch) and Saul. While they were worshiping the Lord and fasting....*
>
> (Acts 13:1–2 NIV)

Earlier, we talked about how worship is the best preparation for hearing the Lord's voice. These leaders from the church at Antioch were "worshiping the Lord and fasting" – they were really seeking God with all their hearts.

*While they were worshiping the Lord and fasting,
the Holy Spirit said, "Set apart for me Barnabas
and Saul for the work to which I have called them."*
(Acts 13:2 NIV)

Please note these words: "The Holy Spirit said...."
We have seen that it is the Holy Spirit who brings the
voice of God to us.

*So after they had fasted and prayed, they placed
their hands on them and sent them off.*
(Acts 13:3 NIV)

We need to pay attention to the words the Holy
Spirit spoke because they are very significant for our
discussion on confirming God's voice. The Spirit said,
"Set apart for me Barnabas and Saul for the work to
which I have called them." Bear in mind that the Holy
Spirit had already called Barnabas and Saul. It was not
the first time they had heard about their commission.
But this occasion was public confirmation through their
brothers, in the assembly, that their call was from God.
That was very important for them. They needed that
public confirmation.

CALLED BY GOD

To gain further insight, let's go back a little way into the
history of God's dealings with Paul. From the time Jesus
first appeared to him, Paul knew that he was to be an

apostle. Paul said this himself. In various places in his writings, he emphasizes his divine call, thankful that his apostleship was not of human origin. In Galatians 1:1, he describes himself in this way:

> *Paul, an apostle – sent not from men nor by man,*
> *but by Jesus Christ and God the Father, who raised*
> *him from the dead.* (NIV84)

Paul knew he was not sent "from man nor by man, but by Jesus Christ and God the Father." It is very clear that his apostolic calling came directly from God. Nevertheless, the Lord confirmed this commission through leaders in the church at Antioch when the Holy Spirit said, "Set apart for me Barnabas and Saul for the work to which I have called them" (Acts 13:2 NIV). Barnabas and Saul had already received their individual calls, but this was public affirmation of them. This account shows the importance God Himself attaches to our receiving confirmation that we have correctly heard His voice.

THREE PURPOSES

I believe the public confirmation of Paul's calling served at least three purposes. First, it strengthened Paul's own faith. I think you will agree that there are times when we need confirmation from others. Many of us are walking a rather lonely road, wondering if we really heard God correctly because conditions appear to be so impossible. The guidance that the Lord has so clearly spoken to us can sometimes seem so far away. But then, in His grace, God gives us confirmation through the body of Christ.

Second, this incident at Antioch validated Paul's call to his fellow believers. It wasn't enough that he knew he was called. They had to know he was called, as well – so they could confidently send him out and support him.

Third, the event emphasized the interdependence of the members of Christ's body. This interdependence is something to which God attaches tremendous importance. We are not to act unilaterally, going out on our own. We shouldn't say, "It doesn't matter what the others do. I know I'm right." That attitude is almost invariably wrong. God wants us to realize that we are members of a body, and we need to depend on one other.

RELIABLE COWORKERS

I want you to notice two significant points about this incident at Antioch. The confirmation to Paul and Barnabas came through fellow believers of proven integrity and maturity. That was very important because it matters whom God uses to speak to us. If it is a believer whose maturity, faithfulness, and integrity is known to us, it makes a big difference. Confirmation from a reliable coworker is much more significant than a word that comes from somebody who may be rather unstable or immature in the faith. Affirmation through such a person is worth relatively little. But when it comes through Christians of proven character and wisdom, it means a lot.

Thus, truly spiritual men do not go ahead unilaterally, without regard to their fellow believers. I respect that in Paul's character. He knew God had called him, but he didn't just move forward, saying, "Well, I'm going. Goodbye." He waited on God with his fellow leaders until the call was validated and confirmed. Then, Paul went out with their support and prayers. Believe me, all of us need to do this when we are stepping out to follow the voice of the Lord.

THREE SPECIAL RELATIONSHIPS

We must recognize that our ability to hear God through others depends, to a large extent, on the nature of our relationship with them. The better our relationship with others, the better we can either hear God's voice or receive confirmation of His will through them.

Right relationships are, therefore, essential for being able to hear God's voice. There are three special relationships through which we should expect to hear from the Lord – three relationships to which the New Testament attaches a message of special importance and sanctity:

- The relationship between pastors and their congregations
- The relationship between husbands and wives
- The relationship between parents and children

Let's briefly look at what the Scriptures say about each of these relationships and what this means for our hearing God's voice.

❧ CONFIRMATION THROUGH ONE'S SPIRITUAL LEADERS

Hebrews 13:7 says this about our relationship with our spiritual leaders:

> *Remember your leaders, who spoke the word of God to you. Consider the outcome of their way of life and imitate their faith.* (NIV84)

The word "remember" here indicates respectful consideration. The biblical writer is saying, "Your leaders spoke the Word of God to you, so have respect for them." Consequently, if God speaks to you independently, in a direct and personal way, it should be very important to you that your spiritual leaders, who have already spoken the Word of God to you, should confirm what God has said.

In vibrant Christian fellowship, it is normal and right for God's people to hear confirmation through their leaders. If I were a member of a congregation with godly leadership, and I felt I had heard from God, I would check with them. If I were to go to these leaders, and they waited on God and prayed, and then came back with a reservation about what I heard, I would take note of it. If their answer to me was, "We don't feel that what you have heard is God's voice," believe me, I would be tremendously cautious about going ahead with that word.

❧ CONFIRMATION THROUGH ONE'S SPOUSE

Wives, submit yourselves to your own husbands as you do to the Lord. For the husband is the head of the wife as Christ is the head of the church, his body, of which he is the Savior. Now as the church submits to Christ, so also wives should submit to their husbands in everything.

(Ephesians 5:22–24 NIV)

Another sacred association in the eyes of God is that of husbands and wives. In His infinite wisdom, the Lord has made the husband the head of the wife – responsible for caring for her and her spiritual condition. I realize that many husbands do not really accept this responsibility, but they are responsible nonetheless. If a married woman believes she has heard the voice of God, it would not be prudent for her to go ahead if her husband disagrees. It would be best for her to have her husband's approval and blessing.

I have known many cases in which women went ahead in spite of their husbands' misgivings. Almost always, the result was some kind of spiritual disaster. This is because such behavior is contrary to God's divine order. A woman can have an attitude of, "Well, no matter what my husband says, I'm going to do it!" That type of attitude is not sensitive to hearing from God. Rather, it is a hard, rebellious mindset – and rebellious people rarely hear the voice of God accurately.

CONFIRMATION THROUGH ONE'S PARENTS

The relationship between parents and children is also sacred and can provide confirmation of hearing God's voice. In Ephesians 6:1 we read,

Children, obey your parents in the Lord, for this is right.

Please note the safeguard "in the Lord." If parents demand that their children do something morally wrong or totally unscriptural, the children are not obligated to obey. But otherwise, children are directed to obey their parents. We must remember that if God speaks to a child, He can also speak to the parents concerning what He has said to their child. If they are in disagreement with the idea, He can also change their hearts, causing them to accept His will for their son or daughter.

There is a twofold application for all of these sacred

relationships. On the positive side, we should expect to receive confirmation of God's voice through the relationships. But on the negative side, we should be doubly cautious if what we believe God has spoken to us causes those with whom we are in a relationship to have concerns or reservations.

Our desire to confirm what we believe God has said needs to be sincere. We can affirm His voice through the several types of confirmation we have discussed in the last two chapters: agreement with Scripture, circumstances lining up, peace in our hearts, and corroboration through special, sacred relationships. When all of these line up, we can have confidence that we are accurately hearing the voice of the Lord.

AFTERWORD
Your Own Journey of Discovery

Throughout this book, we have taken a journey using both Scripture and personal examples to give you a better understanding of how you can hear God's voice. Yet, as with so many aspects of the life of faith, someone else's wisdom and instruction can only take you so far in your walk with the Lord. There comes a time when you must put your hand into the hand of the Holy Spirit and let Him lead you on your own journey of discovery.

We have learned that the one unvarying requirement the Lord expects of His people is to hear His voice. Even though, over the millennia, God has dealt with the human race in different ways, this one requirement and expectation has never changed.

We have also learned that hearing from God enables us to follow Him, and that His voice is personal, intangible, and always in the present. Through hearing specific words (rhemas) from Him in the now, faith comes, and we are nourished spiritually.

The Lord wants us to hear – and obey – His voice. This ability is an identifying characteristic of mature children of God. It produces a distinctive lifestyle in believers as they cultivate the sensitivity and humility of a "hearing heart." Part of the process of humbling ourselves comes through confession – to God and to other people within the context of trusting relationships, as Scripture encourages us to do.

When we begin to hear the voice of God, the critical question becomes whether we are truly hearing from Him at any given time. We focused on four ways that allow us to test what we are hearing, which we can summarize in these questions:

- Does it agree with Scripture?
- Is it confirmed through other circumstances?
- Do we have peace in our hearts?
- Is it confirmed through other believers?

Above all, we have learned that to hear God's voice, we must devote time to worshipping and waiting on the Lord. If we consistently reserve time to hear His voice, and if we come to Him in worship and humility, our hearts will be made ready to receive what He wants to tell us.

Therefore, far from being the end of the journey, this

is the beginning of a new lifestyle for you that will yield untold blessings as you watch your relationship with the Lord grow. The outcome will be the fruit you produce – fruit that will last for all eternity. (See John 15:16.) All these results will come from this vital aspect of your relationship with Jesus Christ: hearing God's voice.

About the Author

Derek Prince (1915–2003) was born in India of British parents. He was educated as a scholar of Greek and Latin at Eton College and King's College, Cambridge, in England. Upon graduation, he held a fellowship (equivalent to a professorship) in Ancient and Modern Philosophy at King's College. Prince also studied Hebrew, Aramaic, and modern languages at Cambridge and the Hebrew University in Jerusalem. As a student, he was a philosopher and a self-proclaimed agnostic.

While serving in the Royal Army Medical Corps (RAMC) during World War II, Prince began to study the Bible as a philosophical work. Converted through a powerful encounter with Jesus Christ, he was baptized in the Holy Spirit a few days later. Out of this encounter, he formed two conclusions: first, that Jesus Christ is alive; second, that the Bible is a true, relevant, up-to-date book. These conclusions altered the whole course of his life, which he then devoted to studying and teaching the Bible as the Word of God.

Discharged from the army in Jerusalem in 1945, he married Lydia Christensen, founder of a children's home there. Upon their marriage, he immediately became father to Lydia's eight adopted daughters – six Jewish, one Palestinian Arab, and one English. Together, the family saw the rebirth of the state of Israel in 1948. In the late 1950s, they adopted another daughter while Prince was serving as principal of a teachers' training college in Kenya.

In 1963, the Princes immigrated to the United States and pastored a church in Seattle. In 1973, Prince became one of the founders of Intercessors for America. His book Shaping History through Prayer and Fasting has awakened Christians around the world to their responsibility to pray for their governments. Many consider underground translations of the book as instrumental in the fall of communist regimes in the USSR, East Germany, and Czechoslovakia.

Lydia Prince died in 1975, and Prince married Ruth Baker (a single mother to three adopted children) in 1978. He met his second wife, like his first wife, while she was serving the Lord in Jerusalem. Ruth died in December 1998 in Jerusalem, where they had lived since 1981.

Until a few years before his own death in 2003 at the age of eighty-eight, Prince persisted in the ministry God had called him to as he traveled the world, imparting God's revealed truth, praying for the sick and afflicted, and sharing his prophetic insights into world events in the light of Scripture. Internationally recognized as a Bible scholar and spiritual patriarch, Derek Prince established a teaching ministry that spanned six continents and more than sixty years. He is the author of more than eighty books, six hundred audio teachings, and one hundred video teachings, many of which have been translated and published in more than one hundred languages. He pioneered teaching on such groundbreaking themes as generational curses, the biblical significance of Israel, and demonology.

Prince's radio program, which began in 1979, has been translated into more than a dozen languages and continues to touch lives. Derek Prince's main gift of explaining the Bible and its teachings in a clear and simple way has helped build a foundation of faith in millions of lives. His nondenominational, non-sectarian approach has made his teaching equally relevant and helpful to people from all racial and religious backgrounds, and his messages are estimated to have reached more than half the globe.

In 2002, he said, "It is my desire – and I believe the Lord's desire – that this ministry continue the work, which God began through me over sixty years ago, until Jesus returns."

Derek Prince Ministries continues to reach out to believers in over 140 countries with Derek's teaching, fulfilling the mandate to keep on "until Jesus returns."

This is accomplished through the outreaches of more than forty-five Derek Prince offices around the world, including primary work in Australia, Canada, China, France, Germany, the Netherlands, New Zealand, Norway, Russia, South Africa, Switzerland, the United Kingdom, and the United States. For current information about these and other worldwide locations, visit www.derekprince.com

PULLING DOWN STRONGHOLDS

As a citizen of the kingdom of God through faith in Christ, you are automatically at war with the kingdom of Satan. You need to recognise this reality, become spiritually equipped, and learn how to fight against Satan's kingdom.

£8.99
ISBN 978-1-78263-720-2
Paperback and e-book

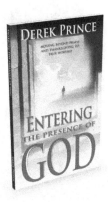

ENTERING THE PRESENCE OF GOD

Derek Prince shows the way to victorious intimacy with God and explains how you can enter into the very presence of God to receive the spiritual, physical, and emotional blessings of true worship.

£8.99
ISBN 978-1901144-42-0
Paperback and e-book

CALLED TO CONQUER

Discover your personal assignment from God. With a thorough examination of Old and New Testament passages, Derek shows you what a calling is, the specific gifts God gives, steps to finding your place in God's service, and much more.

£8.99
ISBN 978-1901144-57-4
Paperback and e-book

www.dpmuk.org/shop

DEREK PRINCE MINISTRIES
OFFICES WORLDWIDE

DPM – Asia/Pacific
✉ admin@dpm.co.nz
🌐 www.dpm.co.nz

DPM – Australia
✉ enquiries@au.derekprince.com
🌐 www.derekprince.com.au

DPM – Canada
✉ enquiries.dpm@eastlink.ca
🌐 www.derekprince.org

DPM – France
✉ info@derekprince.fr
🌐 www.derekprince.fr

DPM – Germany
✉ ibl@ibl-dpm.net
🌐 www.ibl-dpm.net

DPM Indian Subcontinent
✉ secretary@derekprince.in
🌐 www.derekprince.in

DPM – Middle East
✉ contact@dpm.name
🌐 www.dpm.name

DPM – Netherlands
✉ info@derekprince.nl
🌐 www.derekprince.nl

DPM – Norway
✉ xpress@dpskandinavia.com
🌐 www.derekprince.no

Derek Prince Publications Pte. Ltd.
✉ dpmchina@singnet.com.sg
🌐 www.dpmchina.org (English)
　www.ygmweb.org (Chinese)

DPM – Russia/Caucasus
✉ dpmrussia@gmail.com
🌐 www.derekprince.ru

DPM – South Africa
✉ enquiries@derekprince.co.za
🌐 www.derekprince.co.za

DPM – Switzerland
✉ dpm-ch@ibl-dpm.net
🌐 www.ibl-dpm.net

DPM – UK

✉ enquiries@dpmuk.org

🌐 www.dpmuk.org

DPM – USA

✉ ContactUs@derekprince.org

🌐 www.derekprince.org

CPSIA information can be obtained
at www.ICGtesting.com
Printed in the USA
BVHW041517151221
624023BV00014B/1415